MW00612746

קול יוסף חי

HEAR YOUR CALL

MOSAICA PRESS

קול יוסף חי

HEAR YOUR CALL

Fire up your passion for growth

RABBI YOSY MUNK

Transcribed by Shmulie Lazar

Mosaica Press, Inc.

© 2018 by Mosaica Press

Designed and typeset by Brocha Mirel Strizower

ISBN-10: 1-946351-50-4

ISBN-13: 978-1-946351-50-0

Published by:

Mosaica Press, Inc.

www.mosaicapress.com

info@mosaicapress.com

Dedicated in loving memory to my father,
my teacher

Rav Yakov
ben Harav Eliyahu Munk, *z"l*

My father personified the three pillars
on which the world stands:
TORAH—He lived a life of *avodas Hashem* and was
passionate about learning Torah, as attested
by his *sefer, Divrei Yakov.*
AVODAH—He put his heart and soul into his
davening, and, as a *baal tefillah* on the
Yamim Nora'im for close to half a century,
he inspired others as well.
GEMILAS CHASADIM—He was a paragon
of *chesed* and treated each and every person he
met royally, spreading his *simchas ha'chayim* to all.
Together with my mother, *yibadel l'chayim tovim
v'aruchim,* they have raised a generation of
yere'im v'shleimim.
May my mother continue being a pillar of strength
to all who know her, and may she, as the matriarch
of the family, lead us to greet Mashiach,
bi'meheirah b'yameinu!

In honor of

Rabbi Yosy Munk, *shlita*

We feel tremendous *hakaras ha'tov* to you
for the special *kesher* you have with our son
Shmulie, instilling him with so much Torah
and *yir'as Shamayim*.
Your *kol* truly brings much *chiyus* to Shmulie,
our family, and Klal Yisrael.
In the merit of this *sefer*, may Hashem grant you
and your family *shefa, berachah v'hatzlachah,
v'arichas yamim v'shanim, mi'toch briyas ha'guf
v'harchavas ha'daas.*

Motti and Chanie Lazar

~~~~~~

Shmulie,

you had a vision and you made it a reality!
We are so proud of your limitless pursuit of
chesed and *avodas Hashem*.
Your special and unique way of thinking
is inspiring and was instrumental to the success
of this project.
May this *sefer* be a *zechus* to you and Sari as you
embark on this new chapter in your life.
May your *zivug* be *oleh yafeh*, and may Hashem
grant both of you *mazal* and *hatzlachah* in all your
endeavors, to continue being a source of *nachas* to
all of us, the Marder family, and all of Klal Yisrael.

Love, Daddy and Mommy

In honor of

Shmulie and Sari's wedding

Shmuli and Miriam Mendel

Thank you,

Rabbi Munk,

for your constant love and devotion toward me
and every *talmid*. May Hashem continue to shower
your family with lots of *berachah* and *simchah*!
Love,

A *talmid*

לזכר נשמת

Harav Meir Yakov
ben Harav Aaron

Mr. and Mrs. Ira and Rochi Zlotowitz

I would like to thank Rabbi Munk for everything he has done for me. Rebbi has been and still is a great inspiration in my life. I'm also privileged to have the honor of learning with Rabbi Munk, even when overseas. Rebbi has shown me so many strengths and strategies in how to lead my life. Rebbi taught me how to constantly live with *emunah* and to realize it's the ultimate way to lead an amazing life. May Hashem bless Rebbi to have the strength to keep inspiring people all over, whether it's close *talmidim* or anyone Rebbi comes into contact with. May Rebbi have health and happiness and keep smiling until 120.

From a close loving *talmid*

In honor of

Rabbi Munk

The Jaffa Family

לזכר נשמת

Yaakov Yisroel ben Reb Meir Yitzchak Isaac

The love, warmth, and concern that Rabbi Munk has shown me is so beautiful and inspiring. It allows me to keep growing and being the best version of myself. May Hashem bless Rabbi Munk until 120 with continued health, happiness, and being able to do what he does best, which is to love people for who they are. May we share in *simchahs* and happiness together for many years to come.

Love, Menachem
Sponsored by the Herzka Family

In loving memory of

Faiga Raizel bas R' Chaim Beirach, ע״ה

Nachmon and Naomi Simcha

לזכר נשמת

Elisheva Shaindel bas Reb Shimon Aviezer, יבל״ח

Daniel and Amelia Eckstein

לזכר נשמת

Shmuel Yitzchak ben Moshe Aryeh Halevi
Yeshayahu ben Chaim Tzvi Halevi
Bluma bas Yitzchak Isaac

Rivky and Moshe Majeski and family, in honor of

Shmulie and Sari

Avromi and Estee Gutfreund

Chaim and Gayil Chait

Pinny Garbacz

Shmulie Wachsman

Arieh Goldman

Yisrael Meir Fuchs

Volvi Weisz

Danny Krasner

לזכר נשמת

R' Shmuel Krasner

Shaya and Rochel Leah Sofer

In honor of my children, Shragie, Atara, Shlomo,
and Yaakov Meir

Rabbi Simcha Bunim Cohen
K'hal Ateres Yeshaya
Lakewood, New Jersey

שמחה בונם קאהן
קהל עטרת ישעי'
לעקוואד. ניו דזערסי

בס"ד ערב ראש השנה

כאאמו"ר גדול און כיום שורות הללו לכבוד י.ע.ל (פ"ס)
הרב הגאון גמ"ח וכו' שליט"א ... ב"ק ראמ"ו
כ' יוסי שליט"א

עינינו לראות ... אשר ... תורה ודרכה דרכי
הנועם ... עבדכ' עורך לפניכ' ברכת שמים והצלחה
התורה. ורצ... השם יה"ר ... כל שאינו רב ישראל
והרחבה ... וכו' ... אות אל שמחת הבריאת ...
לחיות ולהגדיל ... הגוף ובכל עוד של...

יגדיל ... המעותק דל ועני

שמחה לוני הכהן קאהן

הרב אברהם מרדכי ניסן שליט"א
HaRav Avrohom M. Newman
ראש הישיבה

Rabbi Hershel Puretz
Administrator

Rabbinical Advisors:
הרב ירוחם אלשין שליט"א
הרב ראובן פיינשטיין שליט"א
הרב נתן שטיין שליט"א

Bais Medrash Mayan HaTorah

101 Milton Street
Lakewood,
New Jersey 08701

Tel: 732-367-9900
Fax: 732-358-0336

office@mayanhatorah.org

בס"ד

גאלח גדר דברי הפלשת וגרנה לכבוד הרב ג' יום הכן מונק שליט"א שהולי

נאנר פלצון כבר ש'? כ' שנים והוא אנה של נחור וגחור דרך בחרה יראה שמים

בנ'יאות ובסכלענר ישונה

והני ודגה הוא מומש לאור הקונטרס בפס' קול יוסף ח" על חמשה חומשי תורה

ואוהר הדין קדה לך וצוה ירצה יחפץ מצוה הקל ורן של גבל כום ופרט

בסברו ישנה ובוד מים ודגא לחין ואמינא "שר כח לפפו ובר יהה השר יפה

ואולסים בגנה שילפו מעלה מעלה בחמלות ושרה והיראה לחם ולהם, ויינה למעל אור

דכהם לחולף לא פעים לחברת לם יפל

בברכת כנה והצלחה וכל"ס

ויב ל"ח אמחם ל ב

אברהם מרדכי נומן/

Rabbi Chaim Zvi Senter
Rosh HaYeshiva

באתי בזה לברך מעומק לבי לידיד נפשי הבחור החשוב והיקר המוכתר במידות טובות ומופלג
ביראת שמים ר שמואל נ"י שהניף ידו ציצים ופרחים בהוצאת דברי תורה מאת הרה"ג ר יוסי
מונק על פרשיות התורה אשר פיו מפיק מרגליות בחידושים נפלאים מדברים עליונים ומושגים
גבוהים.

יהי רצון שיזכה לעלות מעלה על במתי התורה והיראה כאוות נפשו הטהורה ולהגדיל תורה
ולהאדירה באדרת התורה

החיתם בברכת התורה,

חיים צבי סנטר

26 Shmuel Hanavi • Jerusalem, Israel • Tel: 011-9722-582-6336 • Fax: 011-9722-6517621
MAILING ADDRESS: Yeshiva Aderes Hatorah • 1072 Madison Ave. • Lakewood, NJ 08701 • Tel: 732-987-7776 • Fax: 732-960-9992

מכתב ברכה

ז' מנחם אב, תשע"ח

My dear friend and talmid Shmuli Lazar has prepared a sefer which includes divrei Torah on every parsha from Rabbi Yosef Munk shlit"a, written in a very clear form.

I would like to thank you for all your efforts in sending out the Divrei Torah of Rabbi Munk weekly, and now writing them up and making them available to the public. I personally have benefited tremendously and grown in my avodas Hashem from the inspiring words of Rabbi Munk.

Reading this sefer, one is struck by the enormous effort evident in it. Shmuli is truly fortunate to have compiled such a work.

May Hashem Yisborach bless you and your family and may you be zocheh to dwell in the tent of Torah always with peace of mind, and may many people benefit from your light.

With much admiration and appreciation,

Shmuel Weiner

Table of Contents

Sefer Bereishis

Sefer Shemos

Sefer Vayikra

Sefer Bamidbar

Sefer Devarim

Yamim Tovim

Foreword

Written by Shmulie Lazar, who transcribed Rabbi Munk's weekly shiurim for publication in this sefer.

When I was in Rabbi Newman's yeshiva, I met **Rabbi Munk**, a true role model. Besides for delivering amazing *shiurim*, he genuinely loves and cares for every *bachur*. Any time a *bachur* needs to speak with him, he is there—listening and ready to give advice. He is everyone's listening ear; not only does he hear the person, but he sees the spark of their *neshamah*. Rabbi Munk is a genuine *nosei b'ol*, and his care for the *bachurim* remains even after they leave the yeshiva. On numerous occasions, he has called me to ask, "How is this *bachur* doing? Tell him to call me," or "What is this person's parents' number? I want to give them a *nachas* report."

It feels like it was just yesterday...Friday mornings I sat in the back right of the *beis midrash* listening to Rabbi Munk's *vort* on the *parashah*, which was always so full of content and yet at the same time straight to the point. I always looked forward to sharing them, and they truly enhanced my Shabbos meals. When I left to Eretz Yisrael, I would call Rabbi Munk once in a while, but I still missed those weekly *vorts*. Time passed, and I came home for *bein ha'zmanim*. I visited Rabbi Munk in Lakewood, and sometime later I had an amazing idea (thank You

Hashem, for giving me this thought and *zechus*), and I called him and asked, "If I give you a recorder, could you record a short *vort* every week and send it to me?" Rabbi Munk answered in the affirmative, and that was the start of the weekly email called "Insights on the Parashah by Rabbi Munk." We started with around ten people, and now, *baruch Hashem*, we have more than three hundred subscribers.

When we came close to the end of the year, I was thinking it would be nice to print a *sefer*. We contacted **Rabbi Haber** and **Rabbi Kornbluth** from Mosaica Press, and they agreed to take the project on. Rabbi Munk and I couldn't have asked for a more professional staff; their creativity and attention to detail is remarkable, and it was a pleasure working with them.

It is very appropriate that this *sefer* is called *Hear Your Call*, because Rabbi Munk hears the true call of the generation. Thank you, Rebbi, for giving me the opportunity to spread your Torah weekly and trusting me to work with your amazing insights.

Thank you to all the **generous sponsors**, for opening your hearts. Without you, this *sefer* would never have come to fruition. May you and your respective families see much *berachah* and *hatzlachah* in the *zechus* of spreading Torah.

Thank you **Rabbi Steg and Rabbi Sender**, my twelfth grade *rebbeim*, for guiding me to grow in *avodas Hashem*.

Thank you **Rosh Yeshiva, Rabbi Avrohom Mordechai Newman**, *shlita*, for giving me the opportunity to forge an everlasting relationship with you. Even after leaving the yeshiva, I am still closely connected, and it feels like I never left. Your concern for me—as for all your *talmidim*—has no limits. Thank you to all the *rebbeim* and *hanhalah* in the yeshiva.

Thank you **Rosh Yeshiva, Rabbi Chaim Zvi Senter**, *shlita*, for giving so much of your valuable, precious time—including for this *sefer*—and for guiding me in so many different ways in Torah and in life. Thank you for allowing me to be your *chavrusa* and for believing in my ability to push for greatness in Torah. Being in your yeshiva has developed in me a thirst to grow in learning Torah and a love for *kedushas Eretz Yisrael*. Thank you to all of the *hanhalas ha'yeshiva*, who have had such an impact on my growth.

Since I was in twelfth grade, I have been listening to the weekly schmooze of my **Mashgiach, Rabbi Chaim Dov Stark,** *shlita.* These have had a major impact on my life and the lives of many others. Thank you, Rabbi Stark, for giving me a tremendous amount of time—guiding, listening, learning together as *chavrusas*—and teaching me how to live my life the Torah way.

Rabbi Shmuel Weiner, *shlita,* who is my *posek* and the *posek* in yeshiva, has been overseeing the *sefer* from its inception and has given invaluable practical advice. Thank you for all the time—and especially for the *zechus* to learn with you every morning for five minutes. My *emunah* and *bitachon* has increased because of you.

Thank you to all my *rebbeim* and *chavrusas* for always being available to learn with me.

Thank you **Rav Gavriel Friedman, Rabbi Gedaliah Zlotowitz, Rabbi Puritz,** and **Dovid Cohen,** for your contributions to the *sefer.*

~~~~~~~~~

When you walk into a bakery, your nose is immediately tickled by the delicious smell of the bread, croissants, and the scrumptious sponge cake. You may ask the baker, "What ingredients did you use for these delicious baked goods? What is it that makes them look and taste so good?" The baker may answer, "Well, sir, there are many different ingredients, and one must also know the right balance—there are precise measurements of sugar, flour, water, and eggs. And most important, all must be done with love!"

Dear **Daddy and Mommy,** the person I am today and my part and *zechus* in this *sefer* are all because of you. You gave me the the best ingredients possible. You ingrained in me, Chaim Yehuda, and Eliyahu the perfect balance of Torah, *hashkafah, yir'as Shamayim,* fun, and all with constant unconditional love. Thank you, Daddy and Mommy, for always being there for me.

Thank you **Daddy and Mommy Marder,** for being the best in-laws ever! It is a true honor for me to join you, **Tamar, Aviva, Layla,** and **Ami.**

There are no words that can fully express my *hakaras ha'tov* to Hakadosh Baruch Hu for giving me **Sari,** who is the greatest gift and joy of my life. May we be *zocheh* to build a beautiful home and family together.

Shmulie Lazar
5th of Elul
Yerushalayim

If you would like to subscribe to the weekly email, please send an email to shmulielazar1234@gmail.com with the words "Add me" in the subject line.

Preface

Rav Mordechai Schwab, *zt"l*, who was my *mashgiach*, used to tell us that when his *rebbi* Rav Boruch ber Leibowitz, *zt"l*, would speak publicly to his *talmidim*, he would say, "I am speaking to *mevakshei Hashem*, those who are seeking to be close to Hashem." For the past thirteen years, I was *zocheh* to learn with the *talmidim* of Yeshivas Mayan HaTorah, under the leadership of Rabbi Avrohom Mordechai Newman, *shlita*. Seeing how the boys learn, observing them strive, and listening to their challenges and their commitment to overcome them has been an eye-opening experience. Our generation is faced with many difficult *nisyonos*, and we at times give up in despair that our youth will not get through them—but we forget that Klal Yisrael is compared to the stars, which appear small from a distance, yet when you get closer to them, you see how large they really are. If instead of talking to our children and *talmidim*, we would use our ears and listen with our hearts to what's on their mind—their struggles, their aspirations, their accomplishments—we would see them up close and see their *neshamahs*—the spark and fire in them—and see how great they really are. We would then start to appreciate and admire them, and they would feel that recognition giving them the strength to accomplish their dreams to grow closer and closer to Hashem, because *"retzonam la'asos retzon Konam*—their will is to do the will of Hashem."

It was in the earlier years of the yeshiva that I started telling the *bachurim* a short *vort* on the *parashah* every Friday—something that related to them and that they could say over by their hosts on Shabbos. It was usually a *gematria* from the Vilna Gaon and others; they were short and easy and brought out the wisdom and beauty of *Toras Hashem*. They enjoyed the *divrei Torah* and looked forward to sharing them with others—you could see how the words of Torah are *mesamchei lev*. These *divrei Torah* were said to each *bachur* on a one-to-one basis; this helped them focus on what was being said and internalize the *vort*. They enjoyed saying it over to their parents, hosts, and friends, which in turn gave them a boost in their self-confidence. Over the years, the Friday *vort* changed to a short, sweet, and amusing *vort* from the *mefarshim* on Chumash.

A few years ago, a young, energetic boy came to the yeshiva, Shmulie Lazar, with a passionate desire to grow closer to Hashem in any and every way. He enjoyed the weekly *dvar Torah*, and when he moved on to learn in Eretz Yisrael, he wanted to continue hearing them. Living in a technological world, he asked me if I could record the *vort* and send it to him by email. As a selfless boy with a huge heart for helping others, Shmulie wanted to spread the *divrei Torah*, so he sent them out to the alumni of the yeshiva and to many others. After a year's worth of the weekly recordings, Shmulie wanted to spread them even further, and the idea to print the *divrei Torah* and make this *sefer* was born.

Rav Eliezer ben Dovid on *Parashas Bereishis* compares the creation of man and his purpose in this world to the game of soccer. In the game of soccer, the objective is for each member of the team to get the ball—which is piece of rubber filled with air—into the goal. In order for this to be accomplished, you need a coach to guide you and team workers to help you along. Man was created by Hashem by taking skin and blowing in air, and the objective of man (the ball) is to reach his goal. But a man needs the help of his coach, his guide—which is his or her parents, *rebbeim*, teachers—and he needs his team workers—his family and friends. I would like to take this opportunity to acknowledge and thank the people who Hashem in His kindness has given me to help me accomplish my goals.

The first of my coaches and guides are my parents. To fully describe what they have done and continue to do for me in all aspects of life, *b'ruchniyus u'b'gashmiyus*, would need a book of its own. My father, *a"h*, was my guide, mentor, *rebbi*, and inspiration. His life was total *avodas Hashem*, his days and nights focused on learning Torah. He viewed all aspects of life in a deeper way, seeing them through his understanding of Torah and his *mesorah* from his father, Rav Eliyahu Munk, *zt"l*, from Paris, and *rebbeim* Rav Eliyahu Meir Bloch, *zt"l*, Rav Hutner, *zt"l*, and many others. His *avodas ha'tefillah* was an inspiration to all, and his *simchas ha'chayim* was and still is our guide for how to truly live life. My mother, may she live in good health till 120 years, was the ultimate partner and recipient of my father's *avodas Hashem*, and, with her overflowing love and selflessness, raised us and engrained those values in us — not by preaching but by being an example for us.

My grandfather, an author of many *sefarim* — *The World of Prayer*, *The Call of the Torah*, and others — joined us for the last few years of his life. Just watching him learn and behave with his pleasant and noble ways, and seeing my grandmother's happy attitude, made an everlasting impression on me, and I thank Hashem that I was able to observe them on a daily basis.

My father brought us up to appreciate all different approaches to *Yiddishkeit*, such as Litvish, Chassidish, Sefardish and *Toras ha'nistar*. He would take us to observe many *gedolim*, which gave us a better understanding of them. I was *zocheh* to learn in Yeshivas Torah Temimah, and then by HaRav Meir Stern, *shlita*, in Passaic Yeshiva, and developed a close relationship with the *mashgiach* Harav Mordechai Schwab, *zt"l*. I later learned in Yeshivas Bais Hatalmud in Bensonhurst.

I met my next mentors and guides, my in-laws Rav Avrohom Moshe and Jennie Possick, *shetichyu*, may they live long and healthy years till 120 years. They have been a guide not only to me but to Klal Yisrael. My father-in-law has lived *chinuch* all the years, helping yeshivos and individuals together with Torah Umesorah, and my mother-in-law, through teaching young children.

Until a man is married, he is like a deflated ball missing some air and incomplete. My in-laws gave me the air that I was missing by giving me their daughter Chani as my wife. Our ball was then completely full of air and ready to roll and reach our goals. She has and continues to give me the ability to learn and spread Torah. She has gone above and beyond to ensure that our home has the *ruchniyus* and *gashmiyus* it needs to enable all to grow and reach their potential. May Hashem give her the strength and wisdom to continue reaching our goals with good health and *menuchas ha'nefesh* till 120 years.

The team that helps a man reach his goals is made up of his friends, neighbors, and relatives. Siblings are an important part of that team, and Hashem has blessed me and my wife with the most supportive and encouraging siblings; we could not have gotten to where we are today without them. May Hashem shower them all with *berachah v'hatzlachah* and *nachas* from their own families.

One of our goals is our children, and we can't thank Hashem enough for the gift of each and every one of them—the marrieds, their spouses, the singles—each one a shining star in their own way. They light up our world and the world of others. Hashem should *bentch* them all with *gezunt,* with the ability to reach their goals in bringing *kavod Shamayim,* and with *nachas* from their own till 120 years.

Where are a person's *talmidim* in this picture?

The Gemara says, "*U'mitalmidai yoser mi'kulam*—A person learns the most from his *talmidim*." The reason for this is because the desire to give over to others causes a man to get clarity himself, and Hashem gives him special *siyata diShmaya* for that. In that case then, my *talmidim* belong to the category of my *rebbeim* and those who inspire me; from you I have learned the most. In all the years that I was in the yeshiva, I saw in each and every one of the *talmidim* the qualities of true *mevakshei Hashem* and a passion for growth. May they continue growing in Torah and *yir'as Shamayim,* realize their potential for greatness, and apply it until they reach their own goals.

There is another goal that one has to reach: the *pasuk* in *Parashas Eikev* says, "*Lo yiheyeh vecha akar v'akarah*—You will not be barren from children." The Baal Haturim says this means *divrei Torah*; the Torah that one is *mechadesh* or clarifies for himself is considered his children. This goal was reached through my *rebbeim* and *talmidim*. May Hashem grant me the *zechus* to continue to be *marbeh kavod Shamayim ad bi'as go'el tzedek*, which is the ultimate goal of the world.

Yosy Munk

Elul 5778

Acknowledgments

אֵין אֲנַחְנוּ מַסְפִּיקִים לְהוֹדוֹת...אֶת שְׁמֶךָ.

There are no words to fully thank Hashem for all his *chas-sadim* for us always. *Hodu la'Hashem ki tov*, for bringing to fruition this *sefer* of *divrei Torah* on the weekly *parashah*. This was not a dream project of years, rather a clear *yad Hashem*, with a tremendous amount of *siyata diSh-maya,that* in such a short time this should come to be.

Mosaica Press is well known in the Jewish world for its expertise in publishing. Thank you, Rabbi Haber and Rabbi Kornbluth, for believing in us and for encouraging the publication of the *divrei Torah*. You truly "heard our call." Thank you, Mrs. Brodie, for designing a most lively and appealing book cover. You have been patient and considerate all along; with the awareness that people judge a book by its cover, you precisely and attractively portrayed its contents. And thank you to the whole staff, for promptly printing the *sefer* in time for Shmulie and Sari's *chasunah*. May you continue to make Torah more accessible to the masses.

Thank you, Rabbi and Rebbetzin Simcha Bunim Cohen, for always being there for our family and always answering our call. May Hashem give you the strength to continue inspiring Klal Yisrael.

A heartfelt thanks to my dear brother and sister-in-law, Yehuda and Tzivi Munk. You seem to know everything about everything and then selflessly act upon it. Your support and advice from the beginning through it all are tremendously valued. May Hashem give you the strength to continue helping the *klal* and *yachid* as you so wonderfully do in a humble way. May you see *nachas* from your special *mishpachah*.

Thank you, Rabbi Avrohom Mordechai Newman, *shlita*, for inviting me to join you in your yeshiva. You have created a wonderful *makom Torah* and have the *siyata diShmaya* of getting boys who are gems; all that is left is to polish them. All these *vorts* are credited to you, for through the *talmidei ha'yeshiva*, they were created. May Hashem give you and your *rebbetzin* the *ko'ach* to continue in your *avodas ha'kodesh*. And may Hashem help you, together with Rabbi Puretz, to spread Torah to Klal Yisrael.

Thank you, Mr. and Mrs. Lazar; all the amazing qualities of Shmulie come from a source, and that's you—his parents. You invested in him, as you do in all your children, a love and passion for Torah and *chessed*, and you have taught the right values in life. You have been and continue to be supportive, in your quiet and humble ways, of everything that Shmulie does and especially of this project. May you and Mr. and Mrs. Marder be *zocheh* to see *nachas* from Shmulie and Sari, as they build their own home, and may you see *nachas* from all your children.

And finally, to you, my dear Shmulie, the mastermind behind it all. This book owes its existence to your foresight and enthusiasm. You amaze me as you amaze others with your power to get things done. If anyone says *I can't do it*, they just have to look at you and see that *Yes, I can!* You have applied the *maamar Chazal*, *"Ein davar omed bifnei ha'ratzon"*—if there's a will there's a way. Thank you for the many hours invested in proofreading and correcting, fundraising and sending out weekly recordings to hundreds of listeners—all done with your wholesome good humor. May Hashem give you and your wife, Sari, all the *berachos* and *hatzlachah* as you build your home together. May you make your trademark on Klal Yisrael with your super special talents, always bringing *kavod Shamayim*.

I would like to take this opportunity to thank all the listeners of these *divrei Torah,* and to thank the sponsors, who wholeheartedly helped make this publication a reality. May Hashem *bentch* you with *berachah*, *hatzlachah*, and *nachas* from your own, and may your passion for growth continue to grow.

SEFER

BEREISHIS

Parashas Bereishis

THE GAME OF LIFE

Rav Nosson Wachtfogel asks, "Why is the world obsessed with sports? What is it with sports that the world is so excited about?" He explains it like this: The *metzius* of a person is that he is a *neshamah* that craves to have a fight against his *yetzer hara* and to overcome it. This is our purpose in this world. Hashem gave us a *yetzer hara* in order to overcome it. This is the essence of a person and what the *neshamah* craves. This gives the *neshamah* joy. People don't want to face or do this fight. But the *neshamah* is craving for that enjoyment. So people look for another way of having this enjoyment on a much lower level. Sports is that type of enjoyment. The same idea. You have two teams. You have to fight the opponent, beat him, and overcome him. Since a person is craving for the real fight but he doesn't do it, people therefore go for that smaller type of fight which gives them some type of enjoyment, which is a little bit similar to what the real enjoyment is. Rabbi Eliezer ben Dovid says a similar idea which he finds it in this week's *parashah*.

He speaks about soccer, in which there are two teams. The ball they use is a piece of skin—leather which is full of air. You take the ball and you have to get it into the goal. This can't be done on one's own. One needs a team to help him. There is also a referee who guides and tells you what you can and can't do, and you have a person by the goal who blocks the goal to try and avoid the ball reaching the goal. But you need to try and pass that block. It says in this week's *parashah* that Adam was created, "*Vayipach b'apav nishmas chaim*"; he has skin, the *guf*, and Hashem blew into the *guf* his *neshamah*. The purpose of the person is similar to the ball. His objective is to get to *Olam Haba*—that is the goal. How does he get there? He needs help. This is your group of people, your friends, your family, those people who are around you and are going to help you reach your goal of *Olam Haba*. This is not enough. We also need a referee to guide us in what we can and can't do; that's one's *rav* or *rebbi* who helps him reach his goal. But in front of that goal there is a block. The *yetzer hara* wants to try and prevent you from reaching your goal. This is life; this is what you need. You need to get past the *yetzer hara* to get into the goal. You need the help of others, you need the guidance of a *rebbi*, and together you'll reach your goal. This is the purpose of a person's life. This is the beginning, the *Bereishis*. If a person reaches that goal, then he has the real satisfaction of life, the real enjoyment, and the feeling of accomplishment of what he is supposed to, instead of us going for the small enjoyment, for the sport. Instead, reach for the real enjoyment of life, gain the purpose for what we are here in this world for, and feel the real joy.

Parashas Noach

DAVEN FOR ANOTHER

וְזֶה אֲשֶׁר תַּעֲשֶׂה אֹתָהּ שְׁלֹשׁ מֵאוֹת אַמָּה אֹרֶךְ
הַתֵּבָה חֲמִשִּׁים אַמָּה רָחְבָּהּ וּשְׁלֹשִׁים אַמָּה קוֹמָתָהּ:

And this [is the size] you shall make it: three
hundred cubits the length of the ark, fifty
cubits its breadth, and thirty cubits its height.

(Bereishis 6:15)

Pasuk 6:15 speaks about the measurements of the *teivah*. Hashem gave Noach the specific measurements of the *teivah*; three hundred *amos* long, thirty *amos* high and fifty *amos* wide. What is the meaning of these measurements?

Rav Yonasan Eibeshetz says that Hashem was telling Noach that his generation was full of *reshaim* that were worthy of being destroyed in a *mabul*. But Noach could have saved the generation had he davened for them to do *teshuvah*. But he didn't. So they had to be destroyed and the *teivah* had to save Noach. The measurements Hashem gave Noach were a *remez* that he should have used his mouth to daven for the generation:

In *gematria*, three hundred corresponds to the letter *shin*, thirty to *lamed*, and fifty to *nun*. These three letters—*lamed, shin,* and *nun* spell *lashon*. Had Noach used his *lashon*, his tongue, i.e., his mouth to daven, there wouldn't have been a *mabul*. This is why Hashem asked Noach to build a *teivah* with these measurements.

Rav Eibeshetz asks, "What did Noach do instead of davening? He kept quiet." The letters that come directly after those in the word *lashon* are *samech, taf,* and *mem*, which spell *sosam*, which means "closed." Instead of using his *lashon*, he kept his mouth closed. What happened after he came out of the *teivah*? Because he did not use his *lashon*, He went down in *madreigah*. He planted a vineyard, took the grapes, made wine, and became drunk. The letters that come directly before *lashon* are *chaf, reish,* and *mem*, which spells out *kerem*, a vineyard. Because Noach didn't use his *lashon*, he went down in *madreigah* and planted the vineyard and became drunk.

At the beginning of the *parashah*, the Torah says that Noach was a *tzaddik*. Later on, it says Noach was an "*ish ha'adamah*." He went down in *madreigah* because he did not use the proper tool of *tefillah*. He davened for himself, but he didn't daven for others.

The month in which *Parashas Noach* is read is *chodesh* Cheshvan, also called Marcheshvan. For most people this means "the bitter month of Cheshvan" because there is no Yom Tov in this month. Others look at it differently. It can be read as "*merachshin*," to mouth or utter. We are coming after the month of Tishrei, which is full of days of many *tefillos*—Rosh Hashanah, Yom Kippur, Sukkos. We were under the awesome inspiration of *tefillah*. In Marcheshvan, we can continue with that *tefillah*—*merachshin*, our mouths are still whispering and uttering the words of *tefillah*; we are still under the inspiration of the previous month. Let it be a month full of *tefillah*, and we should use it to daven not only for ourselves but for all of Klal Yisrael and be *zocheh* to the *geulah sheleimah*!

Parashas
Lech Lecha

SHOOTING FOR THE STARS

וַיּוֹצֵא אֹתוֹ הַחוּצָה וַיֹּאמֶר הַבֶּט נָא הַשָּׁמַיְמָה
וּסְפֹר הַכּוֹכָבִים אִם תּוּכַל לִסְפֹּר אֹתָם וַיֹּאמֶר לוֹ
כֹּה יִהְיֶה זַרְעֶךָ:

And He took him outside, and He said, "Please
look heavenward and count the stars, if you
are able to count them." And He said to him,
"So will be your seed."

(Bereishis 15:5)

I t says in *pasuk* 15:5, "*Habet na hashamaymah u'sefor es ha'kochavim.*"
Hashem said to Avraham, "Look at the *Shamayim* and count the
stars, *va'yomer lo koh yiheye zarecha*—so will be your children."
This story took place when the sun was out. It says later on in
pasuk 12 that the sun was about to set, so this story took place
by day. When the sun is out, you can't count or see stars. So why was
Hashem telling Avraham to count the stars?

7

The *Lekutei Bosar Lekutei* says that Hashem was telling Avraham, "Why can't you see the stars now? The reason is since the sun is out, it is so bright and there is so much light that the stars seem faded." The sunlight outshines the stars. Hashem was telling Avraham, *"Koh yiheyeh zarecha*—This is the way your children will be." Klal Yisrael is a small nation. The *goyim* are vast—millions and millions. Much more than us. Nevertheless, the Yidden are like the sun and the nations are like the stars. When the sun is out, we outshine the *goyim*. It looks like they don't exist. They are not even noticeable. This is how great Klal Yisrael is—*Koh yiheyeh zarecha*.

There was a big *mashgiach* in Eretz Yisrael many years ago and on the day the elections were won in America, he asked one of his *talmidim* early in the morning before *Shacharis*, "Who became the president, who won?" The *talmid* told him who won. The Mashgiach then said, "If you want to know why I am asking this question before davening, it is because we are about to make the *berachah* of 'Shelo asani goy.' I am not only happy that I am a Yid and better than the lowlife *goy*, but I'm even greater then the best *goy* according to the world's view, the president of the United States; I am happy that I am not even that. 'Shelo asani goy'; I thank Hashem that I am a Yid—better than the best *goy* of the *goyim*."

Rav Meir Shapiro brings another *pshat* on this *pasuk*. He says that Hashem was asking Avraham to count the stars, which is an impossible thing. *"Koh yiheyeh zarecha"*—I want you and your children to know that we don't act upon what is and what is not possible. We do the right thing; we do *ratzon Hashem*. If Hashem wants something, that is what we do. We don't look at the probabilities and the possibilities and the improbabilities. Even though it is impossible to count the stars, *sefor ha'kochavim*, we do *ratzon Hashem*. Hashem takes care of the rest. *"Koh yiheyeh zarecha"*—this is way Klal Yisrael acts. *B'ezras Hashem*, that is the way we will act. *"Habet haShamayim ur'eh,"* Hashem will look down at us. We will look up at the stars and do our part and Hashem will do His part. He will look down and see us and take us out of this *galus*. Amen.

Parashas Vayera

DISTANCING OURSELVES FROM BAD FRIENDS

M any subjects in this *parashah* speak about Avraham and his different *nisyonos*. The *parashah* ends off with the tenth *nisayon*, the *Akeidah*. Avraham was ready to sacrifice his son Yitzchak for Hashem. The *Akeidah* was such a big *zechus*. On Rosh Hashanah we remind Hashem of what Avraham was ready to do with his son Yitzchak, and in the *zechus* of the *Akeidah*, Hashem should grant us a good year. The shofar is to remind us of the *Akeidah*. We also *lein* about the *Akeidah* on Rosh Hashanah.

There is a dilemma, though. There are two days of Rosh Hashanah, and on the first day we speak about where Avraham and Sarah have a debate over what to do with Yishmael, also found in this week's *parashah*. Avraham sends Yishmael into the wilderness. We *lein* this *parashah* on the first day of Rosh Hashanah. Only on the second day do we *lein* the *parashah* of the *Akeidah*. What is the reason that we *lein* the *parashah* about Avraham sending away Yishmael? What has this got to do with the *Akeidah* that we *lein* on Rosh Hashanah? The whole *zechus* is the Akeidah. So what's with the *leining* of Yishmael?

9

We can answer with a *vort* from Rav Yosef Chaim Sonnenfeld. He explains the exact discussion between Avraham and Sarah about what to do with Yishmael: Sarah says to send him away while Avraham says he should stay. What are the two sides?

Avraham and Sarah had different views on how to be *mechanech* their child. Yishmael was a *rasha*. Avraham held that even though he was a *rasha*, it was best for him to stay at home around the company of Yitzchak, who will perhaps have an influence on Yishmael and bring him back on the right path. Sarah disagreed. She held it was not worth the risk to Yitzchak's *ruchniyus* to be around Yishmael and that it is better to send Yishmael away. It says in the *pasuk* that Hashem said to Avraham, "*Shema b'kolah*—Listen to her voice, to Sarah." Listen to her voice as the correct way to handle Yishmael, "*Ki yikarei lecha zara.*" Rav Yosef Chaim Sonnenfeld explains that if you want that people should recognize Yitzchak as your child, he should not be in the company of Yishmael. To be around him is too dangerous for your son Yitzchak. Send Yishmael away. "*Ki b'Yitzchak yekare lecha zara*—with the name Yitzchak your children will be called.*"

With this, I understood that maybe we can understand why we *lein* this *parashah* on Rosh Hashanah. If you want to know why there was an *Akeidah* and how Yitzchak was able to be on such a *madreigah*, it was because Avraham sent Yishmael away, and thus Yitzchak was not in his company. Had Yishmael hung around Yitzchak, he wouldn't have been on that *madreigah*. It's only because of this *parashah* that Avraham sent Yishmael away that Yitzchak was able to be on that *madreigah* to do the *Akeidas Yitzchak*. This is the lesson that we learn. That's why it is *leined* on this *parashah*. We have to be careful of the company that we are around and be in the right company so that we can be like a Yitzchak.

Parashas
Chayei Sarah

A LIFE WHERE ALL IS GOOD

וַיִּהְיוּ חַיֵּי שָׂרָה מֵאָה שָׁנָה וְעֶשְׂרִים שָׁנָה
וְשֶׁבַע שָׁנִים שְׁנֵי חַיֵּי שָׂרָה:

And the life of Sarah was one hundred years
and twenty years and seven years; [these
were] the years of the life of Sarah.

(*Bereishis* 23:1)

The first *pasuk* in this week's *parashah* says, "*Vayiheyu chayei Sarah meah shanah v'esrim shanah v'sheva shanim sh'nei chayei Sarah.*" Her lifetime was one hundred years, twenty years, and seven years. These are the years of Sarah. *Rashi* says, "*Kulo shavim l'tovah*—all her years were equally good." This is a little bit hard to understand. Sarah's life was full of troubles. She didn't have children for ninety years. She had the story of Hagar and Yishmael. She had incidents with both Pharaoh and Avimelech. She had many *tzaros*. So what does it mean that all her years were *"kulo shavim l'tovah"*? I saw it brought down that Sarah lived a life like Nachum Ish Gamzu. Everything she perceived was good. Her outlook on life was everything is good and therefore, *"Kulo shavim l'tovah."*

If you look at *Rashi*, it says that her life was one hundred years, twenty years, and seven years. At one hundred years old, she was like she was at twenty-year-old. A twenty-year-old is not considered a *bat onshin*—as having done *aveiros*. Sarah at one hundred was like a twenty-year-old without having done *aveiros*.

The *Sefer Mamtak Mesukim M'Devash* discusses *Tehillim* 100, *Mizmor l'Sodah*. It includes the words, *"Ivdu es Hashem b'simchah."* *Tehillim* 20 talks about *"Ya'ancha Hashem b'yom tzara,"* which we say when we have *tzaros*. *"Bas kuf k'bas kof."* With Sarah, *tzaros* were the same as *Mizmor l'Sodah*. With her, there were no *tzaros*. Everything was one big *Mizmor l'Sodah*. She thanked Hashem for everything. *Ha'kol l'tovah*. That was the life of Sarah.

The midrash says that in this *zechus*, Esther HaMalkah ruled over 127 *medinos*, like Sarah lived 127 years. Sarah's outlook on life, where everything was good from beginning to end—in that *zechus* Esther got to rule over 127 *medinos*.

The word *vayihehu*—with the letters *vav, yud, hei, yud*, and *vav*—reads the same backward and forward. With Sarah, whether her life was going forward, i.e., everything straight, or backward, everything was the same to her. Everything was *l'tov*. *"V'dorshei Hashem lo yachseru kol tov."* Those who seek Hashem are not missing anything. If you look at it as "I have everything," *ha'kol l'tovah*. Like we say in davening, *"She'asa li kol tzarki."* Whatever I need Hashem has given me. I am not missing anything. If I'm missing anything it is because I don't need it. If we have this perspective, may we be *zocheh* to be like Sarah.

Parashas Toldos

KEEP ON DAVENING

וַיֶּעְתַּר יִצְחָק לַה׳ לְנֹכַח אִשְׁתּוֹ כִּי עֲקָרָה הִוא
וַיֵּעָתֶר לוֹ ה׳ וַתַּהַר רִבְקָה אִשְׁתּוֹ:

And Yitzchak prayed to Hashem opposite his
wife because she was barren, and Hashem
accepted his prayer, and Rivkah his
wife conceived.

(*Bereishis* 25:21)

In *pasuk* 25:21, it says, "*Va'yetar Yitzchak la'Hashem l'nochach ishto*—Yitzchak davened to Hashem opposite his wife." *Va'yetar* is a *lashon* of davening. "*Ki akara hi*—because she was barren." Hashem heard his *tefillos* and his wife Rivkah became pregnant. *Rashi* says that *va'yetar* means he davened a lot; he spent a lot of time davening.

Rav Shimshon Pincus, in *Shearim b'Tefillah*, explains the idea behind davening many times. When a person asks for something from his

13

friend and his friend doesn't want to give it, and he asks again and is still refused, after two or three times he should stop asking because it is obvious that his friend doesn't want to give it. The more he asks, the more he will disturb him. With Hashem, though, it is the opposite. He wants us to ask again and again and again. There is no limit. The reason for this is because Hashem wants to give to us. The reason He holds back is because He wants us to ask and He wants us to daven again and again. Hashem wants the relationship between us and Him. When we daven we are connecting to Him. This is what Hashem loves. Hashem sometimes brings us a *tzarah* for the sole purpose for us to daven. He wants that connection.

This is what happened here with Yitzchak. He davened again and again for a child. The *gematria* of Yitzchak is 208 and the *gematria* of Rivkah is 307. Together this totals 515. This is the exact gematria of *tefillah*. Yitzchak and Rivkah lived a life of *tefillah*.

It says later in the *pasuk*, "*Va'yetar Yitzchak laHashem l'nochach ishto.*" *Ishto* is spelled *alef, shin, taf,* and *vav,* which stands for "*Hashem sefasai tiftach u'fi.*" This is how we start the *tefillah* of *Shemoneh Esreh*.

Rav Moshe Shapiro says that the essence of a person is *tefillah*. *Adam* is spelled *alef, daled, mem*.

Spell out each of these letters:

Alef—*alef, lamed, peh*

Daled—*daled, lamed, tav*

Mem—*mem,* final-*mem*

If you take the hidden part of the word *adam*—*lamed, peh, lamed, tav, mem*—you get the word *mispallel*.

The essence of a person is davening—*tefillah*.

Rav Yosef Chaim Sonnenfeld brings another *pshat* why Yitzchak had to work so hard davening to Hashem. *Rashi* says that Yaakov was making *adashim* on the day that Avraham was *niftar*, adding that Avraham was *niftar* five years earlier than his son Yitzchak lived so that he shouldn't see his grandson Esav being born. It comes out that Yitzchak davened for a child, who turned out to be Yaakov and Esav, caused Avraham to die five years earlier. This was very hard for Hashem to do, and so this is why Yitzchak had to daven so much. Rav Sonnenfeld says that the *gematria* of *va'yetar laHashem* is the same *gematria* as *chamesh shanim*, which is 748.

When Rav Aharon Kotler heard Rabbi Sonnenfeld's *pshat* regarding this *gematria*, he said that it could only have been said through *ruach ha'kodesh*.

Parashas Vayeitzei

STONES

This *parashah* speaks about the third of the *Avos*—Yaakov. There are three incidents in this *parashah* that have to do with Yaakov and stones.

The first incident with Yaakov is *"Va'yeitzei Yaakov,"* when he goes and lies down and puts stones around his head.

The second incident is when Yaakov went out to look for his wife Rachel and was standing by the well; there was a rock on top of the *be'er* and Yaakov rolled off the stone.

The third incident at the end of the *parashah* is with Lavan, when he makes a treaty, a *bris*, with Yaakov. Yaakov raises a stone and makes a monument. *"Va'yikach Yaakov even matzeivah."*

Something very interesting; there must be something significant about Yaakov and stones. What is the message and what is the connection?

Rav Shimshon Pincus says that the *Avos* were Avraham, Yitzchak, and Yaakov, while beginning with Yaakov's sons are the *Shevatim*. Yaakov is thus the last of the *Avos* and the beginning of the *Shevatim*. Yaakov is the bridge between the *Avos* and the *Shevatim*. He brings over the *mesorah* of the *Avos* to the *Shevatim*, the *banim*.

The word *even* is spelled *alef, beis,* and *nun.* In the word *even,* there is *alef, beis,* which is *av,* and *beis, nun,* which is *ben.* In one word you have *av* and *ben.* This is what Yaakov is. He is the connection between the *Avos* and the *banim.* This is the *even.* This is Yaakov.

On this topic of stones, there is a *vort* from one of the *chassidishe admorim.* In *pasuk* 29:7, Yaakov told the shepherds who were standing by the well that there is a still a long day ahead. It is not yet the time to bring them in, he told them, there is still time to give them water.

The Admor explains the *pasuk* by saying that the three shepherds by the well are referring to the Beis Hamikdash, which is a spring—the source of our *ruchniyus.* There was a stone on top of the well. The stone is a blockage, which prevents anyone from enjoying from the *be'er,* the springs—the wealth of the Beis Hamikdash. We don't have the Beis Hamikdash rebuilt yet.

The three shepherds represent the three roots of Klal Yisrael—*Kohen, Levi,* and *Yisrael.*

Yaakov is explaining why the Beis Hamikdash is not yet rebuilt, why there is a stone on top of the *be'er.* He says, "*Hein od ha'yom gadol.*" You want to know why the day is long and it is not the time yet to gather in the *galus*? It is because of *hein. Hein* is spelled *hei* and *nun.* Every letter in the *alef-beis* can match up with another letter to equal ten. *Alef* with *tes* is ten. *Beis,* two, and *ches,* eight, equals ten. Every letter in the *alef-beis* can equal ten. Except for *hei* and *nun. Hei* doesn't have another letter to match up with to equal ten. So too, the *nun* doesn't have another letter to add to it to equal one hundred. They only have themselves—a *hei* with a *hei* or a *nun* with a *nun.* Those two letters that can't match up are like two people. Two people who can't match up with each other is a problem that is holding back the *geulah.* We don't connect with each other. Connecting is not with somebody who is the same like you, but with someone who is different. A *hei* and a *hei* is not connection. *Shalom* is when you get along with a person who is not like you. If you have this *shalom,* then Mashiach will come, there will be a Beis Hamikdash, and the stone will be removed from the *be'er* and we will be *zocheh* to enjoy from the *be'er* of the Beis Hamikdash.

Parashas Vayishlach

EISAV OUR FRIEND, EISAV OUR ENEMY

This *parashah* speaks about the fight Yaakov had with the *Sar shel Esav*. He was struggling with him until *alos ha'shachar*. The *malach* saw he could not win over Yaakov and Yaakov asked for a *berachah*. Then Yaakov says, "*Va'yishal Yaakov va'yomer hagida na shemecha.*" He asked the *Sar shel Esav*, "Tell me your name." The *Saar* answered, "Why are you asking me my name?" It seems from the *pasuk* that the *Sar* didn't answer Yaakov's question. Rav Shabsi Yudelevitz says that Yaakov was asking the *Sar shel Esav*, which is the *yetzer hara*, "What is your name? How do you define yourself?" The *malach* answered, "My name is '*Lamah zeh tishal lishmi*—Why are you asking my name,' why are you asking questions?" The definition of the *yetzer hara* is "don't ask questions." Live in the dark. Do as you feel. This is how I get people to do *aveiros*.

I once heard from my father, *zt"l*, who heard from his father that this is the difference between our *batei midrashim*, our shuls, and *l'havdil*, the church of the *goyim*. Our shuls are built with very straight walls and a lot of light. The churches are odd-shaped and very dark inside.

This is the difference between us and the *goyim*. The life of a *goy* is very obscured, dark, and unclear, and therefore they are able to do whatever they want. We have a very clear, defined bright light and our life is clear. This is really what the *Sar shel Esav* is. This whole story took place by night before *alos ha'shachar*—when everything is dark. This is when the *Sar shel Esav* is able to do his job.

Rav Elazar Menachem Shach says of "*Lamah zeh tishal lishmi*," that a name defines the essence of the thing. The *yetzer hara* has no name. There is no reality to it. It is all fake and obscured. An illusion. Yaakov was able to win over the *yetzer hara*. If we look at what happened right before this fight, it says, "*Va'yevaser Yaakov levado*," he was alone. He went back for some small jugs. The midrash says that because he went back for *pachim ketanim*, he will be rewarded years later in the times of the Chashmona'im, in the time of Chanukah, and be *zocheh* to the jars of pure oil. Oil is for light. Light is clarity. Yaakov had the answer to the power of Esav. When we come with clarity, the light of Torah and *menorah*, then we are able to overpower the *yetzer hara*. That was how he was able to win.

We should be *zocheh* to the light and clarity of the Torah and *menorah* and be *zocheh* to win over the *yetzer hara* and be *zocheh* to the light of Mashiach.

Parashas Vayeshev

SEE HOW IT ALL CONNECTS

This *parashah* has 112 *pesukim*. The *Rokeach* points out that every single *pasuk* in this week's *parashah* starts off with a *vav* except for eight *pesukim*. The *Rokeach* explains that this week's *parashah* is full of the *tzaros* that Yaakov had in his life—with the brothers who hated Yosef, the selling of Yosef, Yehudah and Tamar, Dinah, *eishes Potiphar*. Yaakov went through one *tzarah* after another in this week's *parashah*.

The letter *vav* has a meaning of *vai*—woe. A pain. This *parashah* is full of the pains of Yaakov except for eight *pesukim*. The *Rokeach* says that is for the eight days of *milah*. In the *zechus* of *milah*, Yaakov was able to endure through the *tzaros*.

Perhaps we can explain this in a different way. Maybe the eight is because of the eight days of Chanukah that normally fall out on these *parshiyos* of *Vayeishev* or *Mikeitz*. Chanukah is celebrated in the dark of *galus*, in the night. In the dark times, when we don't see Hashem and we have to look for Hashem and find Him, and we have to lighten up the *galus*. We light the lights of the *menorah* for us to understand how through the *galus*, the *yad Hashem* is taking care of us. When we have difficulties in life and we don't understand it, we have to realize that it is all created *min Hashem* and part of His plan and all connected.

Vav means "and," which connects two things. The letter *vav* is shaped like a hook. A hook holds one thing onto another. A person can look at events and think it is one *tzarah* after another, one difficulty after another. We have to realize they are all part of Hashem's plan and all connected. That *vav* connects them. A person can look at this *galus* and say, "*Vai*," but really if one understands the lesson of Chanukah—that Hashem is behind everything and it is all connected—it turns that *vai* into the *vav* which connects. That is why we have the whole *parashah* of *vavs* save for eight, because those are the eight days of Chanukah, and through them we can see how everything is connected. When we see a dreidel spinning, we know that obviously someone spun it or else it wouldn't be spinning. When we see events happening in life to ourselves or around the world, we have to realize it is the One Above who is turning and making all these events happen. This is the lesson that we learn from Chanukah.

Parashas Mikeitz

LIGHT BEHIND THE DARKNESS

Ⅰn this week's *parashah*, Pharaoh had a dream and he couldn't find anyone to interpret it. Comes along the *Sar HaMashkim* and he says that when he was in prison there was another prisoner there, Yosef, who had interpreted his dream. The *pasuk* then says, "*Va'yehi ka'asher posar lanu*," the way he interpreted our dream is the way it actually happened.

My grandfather, Rabbi Eliyahu Munk, in his *sefer* on *Chumash*, says that from here the Gemara says that all dreams and the way a person interprets his dreams is the way that the dream will play itself out. But not only that—this rule applies to everything in life. In all situations in life, there is no reality. The way we perceive it is the way it is. If a person is optimistic and positive and he takes the situation in the right way, that's the way it is. If he is negative, then that is the way it is. All of life depends on the person's outlook on the situation he has.

"*Chacham einav b'rosho*—a wise man's eyes are in his head." What does this mean? His eyes are on his face? When a wise person sees something, he doesn't see it at face value for what it is; he interprets

22

what he sees. If he is smart, he will interpret it in the right way, in the positive way. His eyes are, so to speak, in his head because what he sees is not the way it is. It all depends on how he looks at it, and that he looks at it in the right way.

The famous example is half a cup full of water—do you see it as half empty or as half full? The wise person looks at the cup and says that it is half full. *Chacham* is spelled *ches, chaf,* and *mem. Ches* is for *chetzi, chaf* is for *kos,* and *mem* is for *malei.* Half the cup is full. The wise man is able to see that half the cup is full.

When the Chashmona'im came to the Beis Hamikdash and saw that it was totally destroyed, they only found one jug of oil. Not enough to last for eight days. They could have said, "That's it, there isn't enough." They could have looked at what was missing. But they didn't look at it that way. They saw what there is—they saw that half the jug was full. There is what to work with over here. They used that cup and that is why we are *zocheh* to an eight-day Yom Tov. *"B'nei binah yemei shemonah,"* they were *b'nei binah,* they were *chachamim,* and because of that we have the eight days of Chanukah.

The Yom Tov of Chanukah is *"l'hodos u'l'hallel,"* to thank Hashem for all the good that there is. If we look at the situations in life negatively and focus on what is missing in life, then we won't come to thank Hashem, because what do we have to thank Him for when "I am missing this and missing that..."? If we are *chachamim* and we look at what we have and appreciate it, then we will take this Yom Tov and we will thank Hashem for everything that He gives us and we will be able to use the Yom Tov to its fullest.

We say in *Haneros Halalu, "Ein lanu reshus l'hishtamesh bahem ela lirosom bilvad*—We cannot use the *neiros,* we may only look at them, *kedei l'hodos u'l'hallel."* Let our look be the look of the *chacham* whose *"einav b'rosho."* He looks at the positive and all the good Hashem gives us. Why? *Kedei l'hodos u'l'hallel,* we will thank and praise Hashem.

A *freilichin Chanukah.*

Parashas Vayigash

THE BEIS HAMIKDASH CONNECTS HEAVEN AND EARTH

When Yaakov meets Yosef for the first time after twenty-two years, the *pasuk* says, "*Va'yipol al tzavarav va'yivke al tzavaro.*" Yosef fell on Yaakov's neck and he cried on his neck. *Rashi* says Yaakov did not fall on Yosef's neck because Yaakov was saying *Krias Shema*. The interesting thing here is the place that Yosef fell was not on Yaakov's shoulder but on his neck. Earlier in the *parashah*, Yosef meets Binyamin for the first time. He fell on Binyamin's neck and cried, and Binyamin fell on his neck.

Rashi asks, why did he cry on his neck? Yosef cried because Binyamin would have the Beis Hamkidash built in his *chelek* in Eretz Yisrael, which would be destroyed, and therefore he cried. Again it was by the neck.

What is the significance of the neck? Rav Shlomo Levenstein explains in his *sefer* that in *Shir HaShirim*, the Beis Hamikdash is compared to the neck: "*K'migdal David tzavarech.*" The neck is the part of the body that connects the head to the rest of the body. The head is the place where the *ruchniyus* is, the *neshamah* is, and where we breathe. This all comes from the head and travels through the neck, which connects the head, the *ruchniyus*, to the rest of the body, the *gashmiyus*. That connection is done through the neck. The Beis Hamikdash is the place where Klal Yisrael connects with Hashem. The *Shechinah* rests in the Beis Hamikdash, Klal Yisrael comes there, and the connection happens through the Beis Hamikdash. Therefore, the Beis Hamikdash is compared to the neck.

When Yaakov met Yosef for the first time after twenty-two years, after waiting anxiously to see Yosef, the love for Yosef was at its peak. At that moment Yaakov took the natural love that a father has for his son and he channeled it for the love of Hashem and he said *Krias Shema*. This is like the Beis Hamikdash, where the connection of *Shamayim* and *eretz* happens. This is what Yaakov did. He was an epitome of a *mikdash me'at*. Therefore, Yosef fell on Yaakov's neck because Yaakov symbolized the neck, the Beis Hamikdash, which is that connection. When Yosef met Binyamin, they cried on each other's necks because they were thinking about the Beis Hamikdash, which is the neck. Not only that, but Yosef and Binyamin wanted to show us how to rebuild the Beis Hamikdash, which was destroyed because of *sinas chinam*. Yosef was thinking about the *tza'ar* of Binyamin, his Beis Hamikdash, which was built in his *chelek*. Binyamin was thinking about Yosef's *tza'ar*, the *Mishkan Shiloh*, which was built in his *chelek*. Each one was thinking of the other's *tza'ar* and not their own. This is the epitome of *ahavas chinam*. That was what they were trying to tell us with this connection of crying on the neck.

Asarah b'Teves, which usually occurs during the time of year this *parashah* is read, is the beginning of the process that led to the destruction of the Beis Hamikdash. At this point, *Parashas Vayigash*, we should take the message of *ahavas chinam*, of thinking about others and not about ourselves, and may we be *zocheh* instead to the *binyan* of the Beis Hamikdash.

Parashas Vayechi

BRING MY CHILDREN CLOSE

וַיַּרְא יִשְׂרָאֵל אֶת בְּנֵי יוֹסֵף וַיֹּאמֶר מִי אֵלֶּה:
וַיֹּאמֶר יוֹסֵף אֶל אָבִיו בָּנַי הֵם אֲשֶׁר נָתַן לִי אֱלֹקִים
בָּזֶה וַיֹּאמַר קָחֶם נָא אֵלַי וַאֲבָרֲכֵם:

Then Yisrael saw Yosef's sons, and he said,
"Who are these?" Yosef said to his father,
"They are my sons, whom Hashem gave me
here." So he said, "Now bring them near to
me, so that I may bless them."

(Bereishis 48:8–9)

I t says in the *parashah,* *"Va'yar Yisrael es b'nei Yosef va'yomer mi eleh va'yomer Yosef banai heim."*

Yaakov saw the sons of Yosef and he said, "Who are they?" Yosef said, "They are my children." Yaakov replied, "Bring them to me and I will bless them."

Rabbi Paysach Krohn tells a story. Rabbi Ronnie Greenwald was very much into being *mekarev* kids. Once he was working, and there were three *chassidishe bochurim* who had left yeshiva and were working in the same business as him. He decided that he wanted to make a learning *seder* with them once a week. One day, one of the boys said, "I want to tell you a *vort* that I heard on this week's *parashah*: When Yaakov saw Menasheh and Efraim, he said '*Mi eleh*'—he didn't recognize them. He couldn't relate to them because he saw that *reshaim* were going to be descended from him. So he said, '*Mi eleh*.' Yosef said, 'These are my children.' What then was Yaakov's response? He said that even though I can't relate to them, understand them, or know where they are coming from, I still want them close to me. He was *mekarev* them. He asked them to come close and he gave them a *berachah*."

Ronnie Greenwald heard this boy's *vort* and really liked it, so he repeated it to a person who came to him, who happened to be a big speaker. This speaker also liked it, so he said it in a speech in front of thousands of people. It got back to this boy that this *vort* that he said had spread to so many people. Two weeks later this boy told Ronnie, "I have decided that maybe I want to go back to yeshiva." The encouragement that this boy had from hearing that his *vort* went so far, this love that he felt was able to bring him back.

This is exactly what Yaakov did. Even though he wasn't able to understand them, by showing them love he was able to bring them close.

After being back in Eretz Yisrael after twenty-seven years, there are a couple of interesting things I've noticed. Back then, when I wanted to phone home, I had to remember we were always seven hours ahead. They are behind while we are ahead. So I had this feeling that just by being in Eretz Yisrael, I am ahead of all those people in *chutz l'aretz*. This is something very meaningful whether we realize it or not. We don't always realize the *kedushah* in this land and how much power there is here. It's in every step we take when we walk around. This is a feeling I wanted to share with the *olam*. *Baruch Hashem*, I have the *zechus* to be here in Eretz Yisrael and I want to thank those who have helped me to be here. We should all be *zocheh* to be able to stay in Eretz Yisrael and greet Mashiach *tzidkeinu*.

SEFER

SHEMOS

Parashas Shemos

HOW TO BE A LEADER OF KLAL YISRAEL

וַיַּעַן מֹשֶׁה וַיֹּאמֶר וְהֵן לֹא יַאֲמִינוּ לִי וְלֹא יִשְׁמְעוּ
בְּקֹלִי כִּי יֹאמְרוּ לֹא נִרְאָה אֵלֶיךָ ה':

Moshe answered and said, "Behold they will
not believe me, and they will not heed my
voice, but they will say, 'Hashem has not
appeared to you.'"

(*Shemos* 4:1)

Moshe tells Hashem that Klal Yisrael will not believe him—that they are lacking in *emunah*. "*Va'yaan Moshe va'yomer v'hein lo yaaminu li v'lo yishmeu l'koli.*" What should I do? Hashem answers, "*Va'yomer eilav...mah zeh b'yadecha*—What is this that you have in your hand?" Moshe says, "It is a staff." The word "*mah zeh*" is actually spelled *mem, zayin,* and *hei—mi'zeh*, "From this that is in your

31

hand." Hashem was answering Moshe: If you have a problem that Klal Yisrael won't believe in you, the solution will come from this that you are holding in your hand, which Moshe says is a *mateh*, a staff. *Mateh* is a *lashon* of "to lean." One can lean a staff either upward or downward. Hashem said to Moshe, "Take that staff and throw it to the ground." If you are going to give up on Klal Yisrael who are lacking in *emunah*, then it turns into a snake, causing Moshe to run away. If you give up on them and leave them alone, that is what happens.

But if you take that staff and stretch out your hand and grab onto Klal Yisrael, who are lacking in *emunah*, then you don't let go of them. "*Va'yishlach yado va'yechazek bo.*" This gives them the *chizuk*. Then their *emunah* will be strong. You take the stick. You have two ways of dealing with Klal Yisrael who are lacking *emunah*. If you leave go of them and throw them to the ground, you give up on them and they turn into a *nachash*. But if you hold onto them and help them up, and give them that *chizuk*, they will be strong in their *emunah*.

Moshe had the qualities of being a real leader. When Moshe grew up, "*va'yeitzei el echav*—he went out to his brothers," to see how they were doing, "*va'yar b'sivlosam.*" He sees their suffering. *Rashi* says that Moshe looked to see what they needed. He felt their pain. He was the ideal leader of Klal Yisrael. He didn't sit back. He went out and felt their pain. He was able to have the *koach* of truly being the *manhig* of Klal Yisrael.Where did he get this strength from? He got this *koach* from Basya who found him in the water. She called him Moshe. Why? "*Ki min ha'mayim mishisihu.*" Basya was trying to infuse Moshe with the qualities of being a leader by calling him Moshe, which means to draw and take out. Constantly hearing his name reminded him that he had that *koach* to be able to take them out from the *galus*. He was infused with this *koach* and became the leader of Klal Yisrael. Moshe always walked around with the *mateh* to remind him of the qualities of a *manhig*—to come out to Klal Yisrael, to hold onto them and be *mechazek* them that they should have the *koach*.

Parashas Va'eira

TWO KINDS OF MECHITZOS

הִנְנִי מַמְטִיר כָּעֵת מָחָר בָּרָד כָּבֵד מְאֹד אֲשֶׁר לֹא
הָיָה כָמֹהוּ בְּמִצְרַיִם לְמִן הַיּוֹם הִוָּסְדָה וְעַד עָתָּה:

Behold, I am going to rain down at this time
tomorrow a very heavy hail, the likes of
which has never been in Mitzrayim from the
day of its being founded until now.

(*Shemos* 9:18)

Amid the plague of *Barad*, in *pasuk* 9:18, it says, "*Hineni mamtir ka'eis machar*—I am going to have it hail at this time tomorrow." *Rashi* says that Moshe Rabbeinu made a scratch on the wall for Pharaoh and said that when the sun will reach that point tomorrow, the hail will fall. It seems from this *Rashi* that the hail fell when the sun was out and there were no clouds. What is the reason that it rained hail without clouds?

33

Rav Shimshon Pincus says that there are two types of *mechitzos*, separations. One type is that which creates distance—it separates. The other *mechitzah* brings one closer to the other. At Har Sinai when Hashem gave us the Torah, He wanted to come close to us. In order to do so, He had to create a *mechitzah*, clouds, so that He could get close to us. A *mechitzah* in shul is for women to be able to come and daven. Hashem wants women to come to shul, to get close to Him. In order to enable this, there has to be a *mechitzah*. This is a *mechitzah* of closeness. When it rains, it is a sign that Hashem is showering us with *berachah* and coming close to us. In order for Hashem to come close to us, He needs that *mechitzah*. This is why there are clouds when it rains. Since Hashem is coming close to us and giving us the *berachah*, we need to have the clouds.

During the plague of *Barad*, it rained. It wasn't a *berachah*, but a *klalah*, so there was no reason to have clouds. Therefore the *barad* rained down without clouds. Perhaps this is the reason why Moshe Rabbeinu made this mark on the wall, *davka* to show Mitzrayim that they are different from Klal Yisrael. We can have walls and it brings us close. But with Mitzrayim, the walls are just to distance and separate themselves. This is why during the *barad*, only those who stayed within the house, i.e., enclosed within the *mechitzah* of their house, were saved. The *mechitzos* in Mitzrayim are only separation. The word Mitzrayim starts with a *mem* and ends with a final-*mem*—enclosed on all four sides. Mitzrayim is constrained. Their *mechitzos* are only for separation. With Klal Yisrael, though, we can have a *mechitzah* that brings us closer to Hashem. When Chazal make *gedarim*, fences, it is not to constrain and distance us but to bring us closer to Hashem and utilize them correctly.

Parashas Bo

BRAZEN DOGS THAT HUMBLED THEMSELVES

וְהָיְתָה צְעָקָה גְדֹלָה בְּכָל אֶרֶץ מִצְרַיִם אֲשֶׁר כָּמֹהוּ לֹא נִהְיָתָה
וְכָמֹהוּ לֹא תֹסִף: וּלְכֹל בְּנֵי יִשְׂרָאֵל לֹא יֶחֱרַץ כֶּלֶב לְשֹׁנוֹ לְמֵאִישׁ
וְעַד בְּהֵמָה לְמַעַן תֵּדְעוּן אֲשֶׁר יַפְלֶה ה' בֵּין מִצְרַיִם וּבֵין יִשְׂרָאֵל:

And there will be a great cry throughout the entire land
of Mitzrayim, such as there never has been and such
as there shall never be again. But to all the B'nei Yisrael,
not one dog will whet its tongue against either man or
beast, in order that you shall know that Hashem will
separate between the Egyptians and between Yisrael.

(Shemos 11:6–7)

"**U**'*l'chol b'nei Yisrael lo yecheratz kelev leshono.*" At
the point of *Makkas Bechoros*, the dogs did not
bark at Klal Yisrael.

How should we understand this? Rav Yitzchak
Hutner explains that in Chazal, the dog is known
as an arrogant animal, in particular with chutzpah. The Gemara says that

35

the generation before Mashiach is going to look like a dog in terms of arrogance and chutzpah. Contrary to what we think, Rav Hutner says that the chutzpah and arrogance of a dog is not that it barks and bites people. Rather, their arrogance is from the dog being man's best friend. This means that the man and the dog are on the same level. That is the chutzpah of the dog—that it feels that it is on the same level as the human.

How can this be? Because humans don't look at themselves as any better than animals. That will be the generation before Mashiach, where people are on such a low *madreigah* that they don't value themselves as anything different than the animal world. At the time of *yetzias Mitzrayim*, the dogs realized the *chashivus* of Klal Yisrael and realized that they were on such a high level. They didn't bark out of respect for Klal Yisrael because they realized how special a nation they were. That is what the *pasuk* means when it says, "*U'l'chol b'nei Yisrael lo yecheratz kelev leshono.*"

In *Perek Shirah*, it speaks about all the different songs that the animal kingdom sings. The last one is the dog. His song is like it says in *Tehillim* 65:6, "*Bo'u nishtachaveh v'nichra'ah*—Come and bow in humbleness, and praise Hashem who created us." The dog at *yetzias Mitzrayim* humbled itself for Klal Yisrael in realizing who they are. From there we learn humbleness and to praise Hashem for everything He does for us.

Rav Yosef Chaim Sonnenfeld says that we find two *makkos* with animals that Hashem treated differently. The frogs jumped into the ovens and were *moser nefesh* and Hashem saved them—they didn't die. The dogs kept quiet and didn't bark, and their reward was that throughout the generations whenever there is a *neveilah*, a dead piece of meat, we throw it to the dogs as a reward for what they did. The frogs did not get such a big reward even though they were *moser nefesh* and were prepared to be killed. The dogs who kept quiet, though, got rewarded forever and ever. It seems that the dogs' reward is bigger than the frogs! From here we see that it's harder to keep quiet and humble oneself in front of someone else than to throw oneself into the fire.

Parashas Beshalach

RIGHTEOUS WOMEN AT THE YAM SUF

וַתִּקַּח מִרְיָם הַנְּבִיאָה אֲחוֹת אַהֲרֹן אֶת הַתֹּף בְּיָדָהּ וַתֵּצֶאןָ כָל הַנָּשִׁים אַחֲרֶיהָ בְּתֻפִּים וּבִמְחֹלֹת: וַתַּעַן לָהֶם מִרְיָם שִׁירוּ לַה' כִּי גָאֹה גָּאָה סוּס וְרֹכְבוֹ רָמָה בַיָּם:

Miriam, the prophetess, Aharon's sister, took a timbrel in her hand, and all the women came out after her with timbrels and with dances. And Miriam called out to them, "Sing to the Lord, for very exalted is He; a horse and its rider He cast into the sea."

(*Shemos* 15:20–21)

The Shabbos we *lein Parashas Beshalach* is also called Shabbos Shirah. We speak about *Krias Yam Suf* and the *shirah*.

In *pasuk* 15:21, we speak about the *shirah* that Miriam sang with all the ladies of Klal Yisrael. The *pasuk* says, "Miriam called out to them, '*Shiru la'Hashem ki goh ga'ah*—Sing out to Hashem Who is exalted, *sus v'rochvo ramah ba'yam*—the horse and its rider were thrown into the *yam.*'"

Two questions:

1. The *pasuk* says, "*Va'taan la'hem Miriam.*" *La'hem* is in the masculine, while it should say *la'hen* in the feminine.
2. Why does it pick the *pasuk* of "the horse and its rider were thrown into the *yam*"?

The *mefarshim* explain that the women asked Miriam, "It is understandable why the men sing at *krias Yam Suf*, as they had left Mitzrayim and are going to be *mekabel* the Torah. But we women, who are not going to be *mekabel* the Torah like them, as it does not apply to us in the same way, what purpose is there for us to sing *shirah*?"

Miriam answered them, "Why at *krias Yam Suf* did the horses drown together with their rider? What did the horses do wrong? They are innocent! The reason is because the horses helped the rider and are therefore responsible for what happened just like the rider. The same thing is true with we women in Klal Yisrael. The men are *mekabel* the Torah, but the women are the ones who enable the men to learn the Torah, and so they have a *chelek* in the Torah just like men. Therefore we are entitled to sing *shirah* too."

For this reason, she picked the *pasuk* about the horse and its rider because that *pasuk* brings out the point that one who helps has the same *chelek*. Therefore, the *pasuk* says, "*Va'taan la'hem Miriam*" in the masculine to point out that they too have a *chelek* in *krias Yam Suf*, just like the men. Not only that, but it's even greater—Miriam told the ladies to sing and they sung the *shirah*, whereby with the men it says that Moshe sang the *shirah* and the men repeated it after him.

Sefer Nachalas Tzvi says that at *krias Yam Suf*, the *yam* didn't want to split because it had a *tainah*: Why should we split for Klal Yisrael when they worshiped *avodah zarah* just like the Mitzriyim? The *yam* did split, though, in the *zechus* of Moshe Rabbeinu, who did not worship *avodah zarah*. So Moshe was the one who started off the *shirah* and the men repeated after him, because it only split because of Moshe. When it comes to the women, *Tosafos* says in *Maseches Megillah*, it was in the *zechus* of the *nashim tzidkaniyos*, the righteous women, that Klal Yisrael was redeemed and they were *zocheh* to the *geulah*. So in the *zechus* of the women alone, the *yam* split. Therefore, when it came to the *shirah*, they did not have to repeat it after Miriam because in their *zechus* the *yam* split.

Parashas Yisro

TAKE THE INSPIRATION
AND TURN IT INTO A FLAME

This week's *parashah* talks about when Hashem gave the Torah to Klal Yisrael at Har Sinai.

The *Taamei HaMinhagim* says that when parents marry of a child, they walk him or her down to the *chupah* each one holding a candle. What is the reason for this? What is done at a *chasunah* is in imitatation of what happened at *kabbalas haTorah*. When Hashem gave Klal Yisrael the Torah at Har Sinai, Hashem was the *chassan*, who was marrying Klal Yisrael, the *kallah*. At *kabbalas haTorah*, there was thunder and lightning. At a *chasunah*, then, the parents walk down with a candle representing the lightning.

Why is this particular occurrence at *kabbalas haTorah* copied at a *chasunah*? *Pasuk* 19:15 says, "*Va'yehi kolos u'verakim*—there was thunder and lightning." Later on, after *kabbalas haTorah*, it says in *pasuk* 20:15, "*V'kol ha'am ro'im es ha'kolos v'es ha'lapidim*—the entire nation saw the thunder and *lapidim*, the lightning/flame." Why did the term change to *lapidim*?

Rav Moshe Soloveitchik says that according to the *Zohar*, there was a difference before and after *kabbalas haTorah*. When a person is outside in the dark and it is completely black, it is hard for him to see what is going on around him. If a flash of lightning suddenly comes, he is able to see his surroundings for a moment. If a person is smart, he takes that moment to look around as much as he can so that when the lightning is over he will still be able to remember what he saw. He will take the lightning and turn it into a moment of light, a flame, so that it will last longer than just that moment of lightning.

In life, a person sometimes has a moment of inspiration that Hashem lights up for him. A person should take that moment and make it everlasting by turning it into a flame for his life. This is the difference between before and after *kabbalas haTorah*. After *kabbalas haTorah*, Klal Yisrael learned to take those inspirations and make it into a flame. This could be the reason why at a *chasunah* we want the *chassan* and *kallah* to know that as they start their life, there will be inspirations in life, and thus they should seize that moment, make it everlasting, and turn it into a flame for themselves.

In *pasuk* 19:12, it says, "*Ki shamru lachem alos b'har u'nagea b'katzei-hu*—Watch yourselves from going up on the mountain and touching it." The Kotzker Rebbe had a play on the words. He said a person should be careful to go up the mountain and not be satisfied by just touching it. Sometimes we have a moment, and we can be thus satisfied to just stay at that place and not go further. If you have that moment of inspiration, take it and it should be an *aliyah* for you to go further on.

Parashas Mishpatim

SERVANTS OF HASHEM

וְכִי יַכֶּה אִישׁ אֶת עֵין עַבְדּוֹ אוֹ אֶת עֵין אֲמָתוֹ
וְשִׁחֲתָהּ לַחָפְשִׁי יְשַׁלְּחֶנּוּ תַּחַת עֵינוֹ:

And if a man strikes the eye of his manservant
or the eye of his maidservant and destroys it,
he shall set him free in return for his eye.

(Shemos 21:26)

If a person hits his *eved* and knocks out his eye or his tooth or, as Rashi says, any other of the twenty-four limbs of a person, then the *eved* goes free. We see how important the limbs of a person are and if one of the limbs of an *eved* is hurt he goes free. A few *pesukim* earlier it says that if a person hits his friend and he knocks out his eye, tooth, hand, or foot, he has to pay him, *"ayin tachas ayin, shen tachas shen, yad tachas yad, regel tachas regel."* Rashi brings from the Gemara that we don't knock out his eye or tooth but he has to pay him.

42

The Vilna Gaon brings a *remez* in "*ayin tachas ayin.*" The letter under *ayin* is *peh*. The letter under *yud* is *chaf*, and the letter under *nun* is *samech*. *Chaf, samech, peh* is *kesef*. You pay instead of knocking out the eye. On a deeper level, "*ayin*" is an *ayin*, "*yad*" is a *yud*, "*shen*" is a *shin*, and "*regel*" is a *reish*; *ayin, shin, reish*, is *ashir*. If a person has his eyes, his legs, hands, and teeth, all these major limbs, he is an *ashir*.

The *Shmeino Lachmo* says, "*Eizehu ashir? Ha'samei'ach b'chelko*"; *chelko* is *ches, lamed, kuf, vav*. *Ches* is "*cham*," *lamed* is "*lach*," *kuf* is "*kar*," *vav* is "*v'yavesh*." A person who has the inside of his body working—the heat, liquid, and his insides, and the outside with all its limbs—is a rich person. He should realize the *chasdei Hashem* that he has.

We are coming closer to *chodesh* Adar, this week is *Parashas Shekalim*. "*Mi she'nichnas Adar marbim b'simchah.*" How is one *marbim b'simchah*?

The Slonimer says that if a person realizes how rich he is and he is *samei'ach b'chelko* in how much Hashem gives him just by living and having all the parts of his body working, he is to be *maleh simchah* from that. This is the *avodah* of *chodesh* Adar—to be *b'simchah* and to see the *hashgachas Hashem* and believe in Him and see how much kindness Hashem showers him with. This is the *avodah* of the *chodesh*, "*Mi she'nichnas Adar marbim b'simchah*"; to continue and grow in the *simchah*.

Rav Shimshon Raphael Hirsch says that *samei'ach* is similar to the word *tzamei'ach*—*tzaddik, mem, ches*, which means to grow. When a person grows he is *maleh simchah*. May we be *zocheh* to a *chodesh* full of *simchah*.

Parashas Terumah

THE FOUNDATION OF THE MISHKAN IS ACHDUS

כְּכֹל אֲשֶׁר אֲנִי מַרְאֶה אוֹתְךָ אֵת תַּבְנִית הַמִּשְׁכָּן
וְאֵת תַּבְנִית כָּל כֵּלָיו וְכֵן תַּעֲשׂוּ:

Like all this I have shown you, the way the
Mishkan and *keilim* are made, so you should do.

(*Shemos* 25:9)

he question is that the *pasuk* just before this says, "*V'asu li Mishkan v'shachanti b'sochom.*" It already says you should make and build the Beis Hamikdash. Why is there the repetition here "*V'chein taasu*"?

The *sefer Shmeino Lachmo* says that we see throughout the construction of the Beis Hamikdash the idea of *achdus* being repeated again and again; the *aron, ketores, keruvim*: "*Peneihem ish el achiv*—they faced one another." By the *yerios* it says, "One sheet connected to the other." By the *kerashim* it says, "The *kerashim* were connected one to

44

another." We know that a person is a *mikdash me'at*. "*V'shachanti b'so-chom*," Hashem rests His *Shechinah* not only in Klal Yisrael, but in each person. When a man gets married he builds a *mikdash me'at* and the *Shechinah* rests there. The *pasuk* is saying that Hashem says, "Look at the way I am building my Beis Hamikdash. With the concept of *achdus*. You should follow in the same ways and if you do that, I will rest my *Shechinah* with you." So when it says, "*V'chein taasu*," the *pasuk* is saying for the second time, "You see how I am building the Beis Hamikdash, follow that, *v'chein taasu*, and then the *Shechinah* will rest within you."

In 26:24, the *pasuk* says, "The planks fitted together at the bottom and matched on top too."

Rav Schwab says that this is referring to a man and his wife. On the bottom they are like twins, they match. But on the top, "*al rosho*," they are one. Their ideals and goals should be the same, like one. That is why the *pasuk* says that "on top they were one."

We can take this a step further. Under the *chuppah*, the *chassan* puts a ring on the *kallah*'s finger. The top of the *kerashim* were put together with a *taba'as* a ring. Rashi says in *pasuk* 25 that "*etzba mi'kan v'etzba mi'kan*," the *kerashim* were a fingerbreadth wide. Perhaps this is why we put a ring on the finger of the *kallah*, where that connection happens. A gold ring is used to bring out this point, that like in the Beis Hamikdash and *Mishkan*, they were one, and this is how they should be all their life. At the bottom of the *kerashim* were sockets, *adanim*, to support the beams. This, perhaps, is the husband, the support of the house he is building. If a person lowers and humbles himself to his wife and family, then he is the *adon*, the master of the house. If he has that quality of understanding that he is the support of the house, if he has that quality of understanding his place, this support, but yet he is humble, he will be able to build his *bayis* and bring the *Shechinah* into his house and build a *bayis ne'eman b'Yisrael*.

Parashas Tetzaveh

SERVING HASHEM WITH FEAR AND JOY

וְזֶה אֲשֶׁר תַּעֲשֶׂה עַל הַמִּזְבֵּחַ כְּבָשִׂים בְּנֵי שָׁנָה
שְׁנַיִם לַיּוֹם תָּמִיד:

And this is what you shall offer upon the
Mizbei'ach: lambs in their first year, two a
day, continually.

(*Shemos* 29:38)

"**S**hnayim l'yom tamid," we should bring two *korbanos* everyday in the Beis Hamikdash, morning and afternoon. *Pardes Yosef* brings *down* from the *Gaon miLisa* that the first *Rema* in The *Shulchan Aruch* says, "*Shivisi Hashem l'negdi tamid*," a person should always have Hashem in front of him. Always being reminded of Him every day, *tamid*, constantly, as it says, "*Tov lev mishteh tamid*."

46

The last halachah in *Shulchan Aruch Orach Chaim,* in *hilchos Purim,* is that "a person's heart should always be full of *simchah.*" The *remez* for this is *"shnayim l'yom olah tamid."* He needs to have *"shivisi Hashem l'negdi tamid,"* which is *yiras Hashem* and *tov lev mishteh tamid—simchah.* These two *inyanim* of *yirah* and *simchah* have to be *tamid,* "Shnayim l'yom *olah tamid.*" Like it says in the *pasuk,* "*Gilu b'raadah*—happy and trembling." Both *yirah* and *simchah* are at the same time.

A *mashal* for this is when a person wants to dance with his two-year-old child on Simchas Torah. He takes the child and puts him on his shoulder and dances while feeling full of *simchah.* But at the same time, he is afraid because he doesn't want his child to fall off his shoulders. So while he is dancing, he is constantly thinking of his child and that he shouldn't fall. So there is a certain amount of *yirah* at the same time as he has *simchah.* It is possible to have both at the same time. The *simchah* that we have when it comes to Purim by the *seudah* and throughout the day has to accompanied by *yirah.* You are drinking and the *shikrus* is only in order to get closer to Hashem. This type of *simchah* is one of *gilu b'raadah,* a *simchah* together with *yirah.* Only Klal Yisrael can understand this. May we be *zocheh* to be *mekayem* all the mitzvos of Purim and have a kosher Yom Tov.

Parashas
Ki Sisa

HARD WORK

וַיִּתֵּן אֶל מֹשֶׁה כְּכַלֹּתוֹ לְדַבֵּר אִתּוֹ בְּהַר סִינַי שְׁנֵי לֻחֹת
הָעֵדֻת לֻחֹת אֶבֶן, כְּתֻבִים בְּאֶצְבַּע אֱלֹהִים:

And He gave unto Moses, when He finished
speaking with him upon Mount Sinai, the
two tablets of the testimony, tablets of stone,
written with the finger of God.

(*Shemos* 31:18)

Rashi points out that the word *"k'kaloso*—finished" is written without a *vav*. This teaches that the Torah was given to Moshe like a bride, a *kallah*, is given to a *chassan*; as a gift.

Why was it given as a gift? The *Midrash Tanchuma* says that for forty days Moshe tried learning Torah, but he kept forgetting what he learned—he couldn't retain it until Hashem said He would give it to him as a present.

48

We see from here the concept of *"yagata u'matzasa,"* you work hard, but then it is "found," *metziah*—it is a gift. Just like a *kallah* is considered a *metziah* to a *chassan*. A *metziah* is something which is lost and then found. It is not something that you bought. It is a gift, something you didn't earn.

The point is that when it comes to learning Torah, a person has to work hard. Even after the hard work, though, the Torah is a gift. In some ways, it is incomprehensible—and therefore above us. We have to work hard at it, but even after that it is still a gift from Hashem, *"Yagata u'matzasa."*

There is another way of attaining Torah and that is through Shabbos. The midrash says that the Torah was given on Shabbos. Shabbos is a day that was given to us for learning Torah. We are able to attain and understand and retain the Torah we learn on Shabbos because we have a *neshamah yeseirah*. As a result, we are able to learn Torah much more easily and remember the Torah that we learned. This is why Shabbos is meant for us to learn and understand better what we learned.

In essence, then, we have two ways of retaining Torah:

1. through *yegiah*, hard work, Hashem then gives us the gift of Torah, and
2. learning on Shabbos when we are given the present of learning and remembering the Torah.

We should be *zocheh* to utilize Shabbos properly, for *divrei Torah* and all other ways.

Parashas
Vayakhel

ACHDUS

וַיַּקְהֵל מֹשֶׁה אֶת כָּל עֲדַת בְּנֵי יִשְׂרָאֵל וַיֹּאמֶר אֲלֵהֶם
אֵלֶּה הַדְּבָרִים אֲשֶׁר צִוָּה ה׳ לַעֲשֹׂת אֹתָם:

Moshe called the whole community of the
B'nei Yisrael to assemble, and he said to
them: "These are the things that Hashem
commanded to make."

(*Shemos* 35:1)

❝Vayakhel Moshe es kol adas B'nei Yisrael," Moshe gathered all of Klal Yisrael and told them, "*Eileh ha'devarim asher tzivah Hashem eschem la'asos osom*—These are the things Hashem has commanded you to do." The *mefarshim* explain why Moshe told them this now, why he gathered them at this point.

This *parashah* speaks about the *Mishkan* and the Beis Hamikdash. Moshe wanted Klal Yisrael to know that the condition for the *Mishkan* and Beis Hamikdash to remain standing is if we are together, if there is *achdus*. *Vayakhel* means "to gather together."

If we are not *b'achdus*, the Beis Hamikdash will be destroyed. The *Mishkan* symbolizes *achdus* and this is the condition for the *Mishkan* to remain standing. Moshe *davka* said this *"l'macharas yom ha'kippurim*—the day after Yom Kippur." On Yom Kippur we all know we are *b'achdus*. So Moshe Rabbeinu waited until the day after to signify that not only on Yom Kippur do we have to be *b'achdus* but also the day after and to continue throughout the year.

This week is also *Parashas HaChodesh*. We are starting *chodesh* Nissan, the Yom Tov of Pesach. One of the mitzvos of Pesach is to eat matzah.

The *Chasam Sofer* says that the *gematria* of matzah is 135, the same *gematria* as *kahal*. Matzah symbolizes gathering together, *achdus*. Chametz has the *gematria* of 138, which is the same as *chalak*. *Chalak* means to be apart, as in *machlokes*. Chametz causes *machlokes*, for us to be distant from each other. Matzah brings closeness. The reason is that matzah is a piece of dough which did not rise. It symbolizes *anavah*, being humble. Chametz is a piece of dough that rose and symbolizes *gaavah*, being egoistic. A humble person gets along with other people and this creates *achdus*. If a person is selfish, it causes *machlokes* and creates distance between people. Regarding the *korban Pesach* it says, "*V'shachatu oso kol kahal*," the whole of B'nei Yisrael should *shecht* it together, so we see again the *inyan* of *achdus*. This is why the matzah is made in a round shape. A circle is a point in the middle where everything else is equal distance from each other. It is surrounded by a line that connects them all. This shows the *inyan* of *achdus*.

We should be *zocheh* to matzah and to the lessons that are learned from it.

Parashas Pekudei

ONE HUNDRED BERACHOS

וַיְהִי מְאַת כִּכַּר הַכֶּסֶף לָצֶקֶת אֵת אַדְנֵי הַקֹּדֶשׁ וְאֵת אַדְנֵי הַפָּרֹכֶת מְאַת אֲדָנִים לִמְאַת הַכִּכָּר כִּכָּר לָאָדֶן:

One hundred talents of the silver were used for casting the sockets of the *Kodesh* and the sockets of the dividing curtain; one hundred sockets out of one hundred talents, one talent for each socket.

(*Shemos* 38:27)

When the *Mishkan* was built, one hundred sockets were used. The *Chiddushei HaRim* says that this is *k'neged* the hundred *berachos* a person is supposed to say every day. Just like a socket is the foundation of the beams, the foundation of a person, which is his own *Mishkan*, is to say one hundred *berachos* everyday. *Adon* is from the *lashon* of "*adon*—a master."

This week's *parashah* is *Parashas HaChodesh*. There are three things that Moshe had difficulty understanding and Hashem had to show him a picture of what He meant: the new moon, the *menorah*, and the *machatzis ha'shekel*. This is hinted to in Moshe Rabbeinu's name. Moshe is *mem*, *shin*, and *hei*. Mem is the *menorah*, *shin* is the *shekalim*, and *hei* is *ha'chodesh*.

Ha'chodesh ends with a *shin*, *shekalim* ends with a *mem*, and *menorah* ends with a *hei*, which also spells out the name of Moshe. So Moshe's name is *merumaz* in the three things that he had difficulty understanding; *menorah*, *shekalim*, and *chodesh*.

SEFER
VAYIKRA

Parashas
Vayikra

HEAR HASHEM CALLING YOU

וַיִּקְרָא אֶל מֹשֶׁה וַיְדַבֵּר ה' אֵלָיו מֵאֹהֶל מוֹעֵד לֵאמֹר:

And He called to Moshe, and Hashem spoke
to him from the *Ohel Moed,* saying.

(*Vayikra* 1:1)

Vayikra means "to call." When it says, "*Vayikra el Moshe v'yedaber Hashem eilav,*" who called to Moshe? We know that the word *vayikra* has a small *alef.* The reason is because Hashem speaks to us constantly, throughout our day He is giving us messages. It is up to us to realize that He is talking to us. We can think that things are just happening by chance, which is called *mikra.* Vayikra is the same lashon as *mikra,* a chance. Moshe Rabbeinu understood that all the messages in his life were Hashem talking to Him. So it's "*Vayikra,*" with the *alef* standing for Hashem. The letter *alef* is written in small because it's at times that He doesn't make Himself noticeable, that He is speaking to us. So we have

57

to make ourselves like a Moshe Rabbeinu or anybody who can copy him and realize that all these callings are Hashem speaking. Even though the *alef* is small, and Hashem is not noticeable, it is up to us to see that He is calling out to us. Moshe Rabbeinu was on such a *madreigah* that he realized that it was Hashem speaking to him.

How do we get to this *madreigah* of realizing that it is Hashem speaking to us? We need to look at Moshe again. He was "*anav mi'kol adam*—the most humble person." That is why the *pasuk* says *vayikra* with a small *alef*. Moshe made it small, humbling himself, realizing that Hashem could call him by chance. If you have the *middah* of *anavah*, you are able to realize that everything is Hashem. Regarding a haughty person, Hashem says, "I cannot live together with him." A *baal gaavah* does not leave space for Hashem in his life. Only a humble person is able to realize Hashem, and then Hashem can be noticeable in his life. That was Moshe.

Alef can be read as *elef*, a thousand. That is the highest number in the Hebrew language. *Alef* is also the first letter in the alphabet, which represents the lowest number. Moshe was the greatest person, he was *elef*, but he was the most humble person too and made himself like the *alef*.

We also learned this idea from the matzah. Matzah symbolizes being humble. Chametz is when the dough rises, and it symbolizes the *baal gaavah*. The matzah is thin, symbolizing *anavah* and humility. If you have humility, you are able to realize Hashem in your life.

The point of the Haggadah and *leil ha'Seder* is *emunah*. Matzah is called the "*michla d'meimenusa*—the food of *emunah*." It brings about *emunah*. When a person is humble they are able to have *emunah*. The whole *Sefer Vayikra* is about *korbanos*. Bringing a *korban* enables a person to be close to Hashem. Those who are humble are able to come closer to Hashem. This is what *Sefer Vayikra* is about.

At the end of the Seder we say, "*Echad mi yodei'a?*" We test ourselves—what is our word association? When we hear the word *echad*, we should automatically think of Hashem. It shows our *emunah* is ingrained in us if it is our first reaction.

Parashas Tzav

CONTROLLING OUR THOUGHTS

צַו אֶת אַהֲרֹן וְאֶת בָּנָיו לֵאמֹר זֹאת תּוֹרַת הָעֹלָה
הִוא הָעֹלָה עַל מוֹקְדָה עַל הַמִּזְבֵּחַ כָּל הַלַּיְלָה עַד
הַבֹּקֶר וְאֵשׁ הַמִּזְבֵּחַ תּוּקַד בּוֹ:

Command Aharon and his sons, saying, "This
is the law of the *olah*. That is the *olah* which
burns on the *Mizbei'ach* all night until morning,
and the fire of the *Mizbei'ach* shall burn with it.

(*Vayikra* 6:2)

I n the second *pasuk* of this week's *parashah*, it says, "*Tzav es Aharon
v'es banav leimor zos toras ha'olah*," these are the laws of the *olah*, it
is to be on the *Mizbei'ach* the whole night until the morning and
you should have the flame on the *Mizbei'ach*. Rashi says the term
tzav is a *lashon* of commanding with urgency. Why? Where there
is a situation of a loss of money a person needs to be a *zariz*.

The *Kohanim* do not get as much from a *korban olah* as from other *korbanos*; there is a loss of money, therefore they need a special *zehirus* and *zerizus* with this *korban*.

The *sefer Ohr Meir* says that there are different senses of a person—eyes, ears, hands, mouth. A person can control all these senses. "*Chisaron kis*"—*kis* means a pocket or protection. We have some kind of protection for all of our senses. We can protect our hands or hold them back from doing something. We can shut our eyes, close our ears. All of our senses have that *kis*, protection, except for our thoughts. Rav Yisrael Salanter says that our thoughts are free and there is no way a person can protect them. A person has to be very careful with his thoughts. It is "*makom chisaron kis*," so a person has to be extra careful.

Perhaps we can say that the *pasuk* is talking about how a person can protect his thoughts. We are talking here about the *korban olah*, which was *mechaper* for *machshavos*, thoughts. Today we don't have the *korbanos*. The Gemara says that learning Torah is instead of *korbanos*.

"*Zos toras ha'olah*," if you want to have protection for your thoughts, learn Torah. The reason why a person cannot control his thoughts is because his mind is not occupied, causing him to think all types of thoughts. If a person fills his mind with Torah, he cannot have other thoughts. So the *eitzah* for protecting one's thoughts is the learning of Torah. But it is not only that. Our thoughts go wild because we have a certain passion and desire. This an *aish*, fire. This passion was created for Torah. Torah is a fire. If a person wants, he can take the passion and channel it either way; either for a desire to learn and then his mind will be occupied with thoughts of Torah protecting against other thoughts. If not, his mind may be occupied with improper thoughts. "*Zos toras ha'olah*." If you want protection for your thoughts, then occupy your mind with Torah.

Parashas Shemini

HOW KOSHER FOOD AFFECTS US

This week's *parashah* falls after Pesach. On Pesach we had the mitzvah of eating matzah. Now we have *Parashas Shemini* which speaks about the foods we are permitted and forbidden to eat. The foods that we eat have an effect on our *ruchniyus*, the requirement we have to grow in our Torah. These weeks, the *sefirah*, are preparation for *kabbalas haTorah*. The food we eat is an essential part of our growth in Torah. In the *ale-beis*, the letter *ayin* comes before the letter *peh*. *Ayin* means to look, while *peh* is the mouth. We always need to look into which food we are eating before we put it into our mouth. The food that we eat is part of our growth. The *simanim* of certain types of animals that are permitted to us or not are because there are different *middos* of how animals behave. There are good and bad traits in animals. The food or animals we eat, the *middos* they have, transfer into us. If the animal has good *middos* then we get good *middos* from that animal. And if it has bad *middos*, we get the bad *middos*.

"*Derech eretz kadmah l'Torah—middos* are a requirement before Torah," and therefore the food we eat is so important.

The two *simanim* of a kosher animal are that it chews the cud and has split hooves. The pig is an animal that has one of the kosher *simanim*. It has split hooves, but it doesn't chew the cud.

The *Chiddushei HaRim* said that the *chazir*, which has one *siman*, tries to show it off and fool others into thinking it is a kosher animal, even though it doesn't chew the cud. Therefore, the animal is not kosher. That it tries to fool others that it is kosher is enough of a thing. Esav is compared to a *chazir*. He tried to fool Yitzchak with his questions about the salt and into thinking that he was a good person. Even though it was bad, in a way it was a good thing. Even trying to fool someone that you are good shows something. The midrash, brought by Rabbeinu Bachya in our *parashah*, says it is called a *chazir* because it will eventually return to being a kosher animal when Mashiach comes. It will change its nature and it will chew its cud.

We can learn something from the *chazir*, despite its present state. It is brought down that it is called *chazir* because it returns. If you push the pig away from its place, it will always return. It doesn't get discouraged. In the *chazir's* present state we can learn from it not to get discouraged. When a person is trying to serve Hashem and he doesn't succeed, "*sheva yipol tzaddik v'kam*." This is the *middah* the *chazir* has from its feet, the kosher part of the animal. The split hooves, the part of the animal that returns to its place, from there we can learn this good *middah*. It could be that from this *middah* the animal has, it will eventually return to being kosher food, because it always has this willingness to go back to its place without being discouraged—this is something that we can learn from. Know that the foods we eat have an effect on us and help us grow in our *yiras Shamayim* and Torah.

Parashas Tazria-Metzora

SHABBOS – DAY OF TESHUVAH

This week's *parashah* speaks about *tzaraas*, a *nega*, affliction, on the body. If a person has a *nega*, he has to show it to the *Kohen*. He has to be closed off for seven days. If it doesn't go away, he has to be checked again. If it still doesn't go away then after that he becomes *tameh*. Why does he have to be closed off for seven days? Why is the *nega* on the skin of the person?

The *Sefas Emes* says that when Hashem created the world, it was clear to everyone that He was the Creator. After Adam HaRishon sinned with the *Eitz HaDaas*, the world lost its clarity that Hashem is the Creator of the world. After the *chet*, the *pasuk* says, "*V'yaas Hashem Elokim l'Adam u'l'ishto kosnos ohr*," Hashem created the skin of Adam Harishon. Skin is a covering, it covers what is inside. Now the world is covered, we don't see Hashem as clearly. The letters in the word *ohr*—*ayin, vav, reish*—are the same letters as the word *iver*; we are blinded from the clarity of

Hashem. Even though we have skin, there are pores in it. It is possible that if a person looks deep he can still see Hashem. If a person is so far removed from seeing Hashem that he doesn't notice Him, then comes a *nega*—an affliction on their body. Perhaps the *nega* is from the *lashon* of *negia*, touching. The first *chet* of Adam HaRishon happened when he touched the *Eitz HaDaas*. How can a person rectify that? A person needs to go through a Shabbos. In every seven days there is a Shabbos. Shabbos is a time when a person can reflect and see that Hashem created the world. Shabbos is a *zichron* to the creation of the world. A person can do *teshuvah* on Shabbos. A person with *tzaraas* has Shabbos, the time to do *teshuvah*, to reconnect and see Hashem.

The *pasuk* says, "*V'hinei lo hafach ha'nega es eino*," if the *nega* did not change. It is brought down in the *mefarshim* that the words *nega* and *oneg* are made up of the same letters—*ayin, nun,* and *gimmel*. The difference depends on where the *ayin* is. If the *ayin* is at the beginning of the word, it is *oneg*. At the end of the word, it is *nega*. The *mefarshim* say, "*V'hinei lo hafach ha'nega es eino*," if the *nega* did not change the position of the *ayin*, meaning that he did not do *teshuvah* and change the *nega* to *oneg*—Shabbos is the day of *oneg*—then he remains *tameh*.

"*Chacham einav b'rosho*," a *chacham* will make sure that *eino*, his *teshuvah*, will be *b'rosho*, at the beginning of the word, and then it will be *oneg* instead of *nega*. This is through having a Shabbos, a time when we can contemplate Hashem and see how He runs the world, and therefore do *teshuvah* and become *tahor*.

Parashas
Acharei Mos

HELPING OTHERS

P arashas *Acharei Mos* speaks about the *avodah* of the *Kohen Gadol* in the Beis Hamikdash on Yom Kippur.

Part of the *avodah* involved drawing two lots. One lot was for the animal, the *azazel* that was sent to the mountain and thrown off as a *kaparah* for all the *aveiros* of the Yidden. The other animal was *l'Hashem*, to be *misvadeh* the *aveiros* and to get a *kaparah* for that.

The animal that was sent as the *azazel* was taken through the *midbar* by a designated person to bring it to the mountain. The Mishnah *(Yoma* 6:4) says, "Some of the precious people of Yerushalayim would go with this person and accompany him through the *midbar* until the first sukkah." The question is, who are these *yakirei Yerushalayim?*

Rav Daniel Stam brings down in the *sefer Motzei Shalal Rav* that the *yakirei Yerushalayim* were people who gave up their opportunity of being in the Beis Hamikdash and watching the *avodah* of the *Kohen Gadol.* Thousands of people were watching the *avodah*. It was a very spiritual moment. Yet these *yakirei Yerushalayim* gave up this opportunity of watching the *Kohen Gadol* on Yom Kippur to be with this person who was going through the *midbar* alone with the *azazel*, which was not as spiritual as watching the *Kohen Gadol*. Giving up of a person's *ruchniyus* to help somebody else is precious. Rav Stam brings down from the introduction to the *sefer Nefesh HaChaim* that Rav Chaim Volozhin told his son that a person is in this world to help others. This is our purpose.

Sefiras ha'omer starts from the second day of Pesach when we bring a *korban* of barley. It ends on Shavuos when we bring the *shtei ha'lechem*, a *korban* of wheat. Barley is food that is fed to animals, while wheat is food that is fed to people. *Sefiras ha'omer* is a time when we rise from our animal instincts to the *madreigah* of *adam*. The question is asked, why do we count the days that have passed if we are looking forward to Shavuos? We should be counting down the days until Shavuos? The *Chiddushei HaRim* says, "We count how many days we have risen from the level of being like an animal toward becoming the ultimate human being. A human being is a person who is out to help another person. This is the *avodah* of *sefiras ha'omer*, bringing us closer to *kabbalas haTorah*.

Parashas Kedoshim

JEALOUSY BRINGS TO HATRED

לֹא תִשְׂנָא אֶת אָחִיךָ בִּלְבָבֶךָ הוֹכֵחַ תּוֹכִיחַ
אֶת עֲמִיתֶךָ וְלֹא תִשָּׂא עָלָיו חֵטְא:

You shall not hate your brother in your
heart. You shall surely rebuke your fellow,
but you shall not bear a sin on his account.

(*Vayikra* 19:17)

In *Parashas Kedoshim*, the *pasuk* says, "*Lo sisna es achicha bilvave-cha*—Do not hate your brother in your heart." Rashi says in *Sefer Devarim* (22:14) that a person who transgresses *lo sisna*, hatred, will also transgress the *aveirah* of *lashon hara*. Why is it that if someone speaks *lashon hara* it means that he hates somebody. What has one got to do with the other?

Rav Chaim Vital explains that the root of hatred is jealousy. What is jealousy? Rashi is telling us that it is a type of revenge a person wants to take.

The *sefer Ezri Me'im Hashem* says that when Reuven sees something that Shimon has and he does not have, the first feeling is, *I want that same thing too.* The next feeling is, *Really that thing should be by me, and not Shimon.* The next feeling is, *Why does my friend have something that should really be mine. He is actually a ganav.* So the initial jealousy ends up as hatred. With other desires, you want something, and once you get it, the desire is done. With jealousy, even if you would get what the other person has, you would still remain with the hate, because you feel that this person took what is yours. Therefore, a person always has a feeling that other people are taking away what rightfully should be his, whether it is honor or possessions, and he will always have a feeling of taking revenge on other people. The revenge that he gets is when he hears or speaks *lashon hara* about the other person. This way, he removes that person from the position he is and lowers him. This way he feels that he remains with his space and honor. Therefore, he is always prepared to hear and speak *lashon hara* about the other person.

This is perhaps the reason for the order of the *pesukim*. *Pasuk* 16 first speaks about "*Lo selech rachil*," the *aveirah* of *lashon hara*. Then it speaks about "*Lo sisna*," that *lashon hara* happens because a person hates. Following this, it speaks about "*Lo sikom*"—*nekamah*. Jealousy is hatred, which is a form of *nekamah*.

What is the *eitzah*?

To believe that everything is from Hashem and if you don't have it, that's because it's good for you not to have it. Just like if a person would be born with wings, it would not be a good thing that he'd have the ability to fly, rather it would be considered a fault in the person. What he doesn't have is good for him. Everything is from Hashem. If a person has the correct *emunah* and *bitachon*, he would not have the jealousy.

The *pasuk* follows with "*V'ahavta l'rei'acha kemocha*—love your friend as yourself." *Ahavah* has the *gematria* of thirteen. If you love your friend and he loves you, you take twice *ahavah*, thirteen plus thirteen, which is twenty-six, which is the *gematria* of the *Shem Hashem*—yud, hei, vav, hei. If a person loves his friend like himself, then he has Hashem's Name. "*V'ahavta l'rei'acha kemocha*," the *pasuk* ends "*ani Hashem*." If you do that then "I, Hashem" rest with you and *b'ezras Hashem*, we will have the Beis Hamikdash rebuilt.

Parashas Emor

LAG B'OMER—A KIND HEART

In this week's *parashah* we discuss the *sefiras ha'omer*. We count forty-nine days from Pesach until Shavuos, preparing ourselves for *kabbalas haTorah*. We don't count the days that are left until *kabbalas haTorah*, rather we count the days that have passed. If we are excited about *kabbalas haTorah*, we should count the days that are left, but we don't do that. The reason is because we are not counting the days but rather, we are trying to make the days count. Every day is a special day where we are preparing ourselves for *kabbalas haTorah*. It says, "*Derech eretz kadmah l'Torah*," we need to work on our character and on our *middos* to prepare ourselves that we should be able to accept the Torah. The *gematria* of *middah*—*mem, daled, hei*—is 49. We have to work ourselves. In the third *perek* of *Pirkei Avos*, Rabbi Yochanan asked his *talmidim*, "What is the best way that a person can work on himself?" Rabbi Elazar said, "*Lev tov*, a good heart." Rabbi Yochanan said that this encompasses all the other *middos* that his *talmidim* said.

The *Lev Yissaschar* says that *lev* has a *gematria* of 32 and *tov* has a *gematria* of 17. The first time the word *tov* is used in the Torah is when Hashem created light. The thirty-third word is *tov*.

69

The *simchah* of Lag B'Omer is that after working on our *middos*, our *lev*, and we accomplish preparing our *lev* for *kabbalas haTorah*, now we are ready for the second part of *tov*: *"Ein tov ela Torah."* Now we are ready to continue working on ourselves to be ready to be *mekabel* the Torah.

What is a *lev tov*? The *Tiferes Yisrael* says that it is a good heart, a person who looks out for someone else. The reason he has a good heart is because he is full of joy and happiness that he is able to think of somebody else and want to help them. Not only does this help him in his *middos*, but it also sharpens a his mind and helps him get clarity for learning Torah. This is how a person develops himself in getting ready to be *mekabel* the Torah. Perhaps this is the *simchah* of Lag B'Omer. That *chedvah*, the joy that we need to add to our *lev tov*, to make it even better so that we can look out for the other person and through that sharpen our minds and be able to learn better, is the *simchah* of Lag B'Omer.

There is a *minhag* to make bonfires on Lag B'Omer. And perhaps this is connected to the above thought. *"Va'yar Elokim ki tov."* We said that the first time the word *tov* is used is when Hashem created light. We make this *ohr* on Lag B'Omer. A bonfire is called a *lehavah*—*lamed, hei, beis, hei*. The *lev* is *lamed, beis*, while *hav* is *hei, beis*. *Hav* means "to give." When a person gives his heart, when he is so full of this passion to give to others, that is the *lehavah* of Lag B'Omer. The same warmth a person has to give to others, that fire is the light that helps him have clarity in his understanding of learning.

This is the *sefiras ha'omer*; not just counting the days, but making each and every day count, preparing ourselves to be *mekabel* the Torah on Shavuos.

Parashas Behar

SHABBOS – A TIME TO MEET YOURSELF

arashas Behar speaks about *shemittah* and *yovel*.

Rabbi Yisroel Roll explains these concepts. There is a *pasuk* in *Mishlei*: "*V'hanchil ohavai yesh*—I gave to my beloved, existence." The *Zohar* says that the *yud* of the word *yesh* stands for *yovel* and the *shin* stands for *shemittah*. The secret of *yovel* and *shemittah* is that when you work on yourself through the forty-nine years of *shemittah* and you arrive at *yovel*, you have existence and you find yourself. *Yesh* is an expression of possession. Like Yaakov said, "*Yesh li kol.*" *Yovel and shemittah* are the concept of having and we arrive at the state of reality, of being. We move away from *chomer*, doing, to *tzurah*, being. Hashem has given us the gift and opportunity to connect with His reality. It is much more than having things. We have this concept with every Shabbos. During the week, a person is involved with shaping the external world. On Shabbos, we have to let go of the materialism and focus on the *tzurah*—who we really are. You can't find your true self without working on your inner awareness. By removing the physical, which distracts you, you are able to come to your *tzurah*, your real purpose in this world.

This is the true reason why the secular world objects to keeping Shabbos. Shabbos is twenty-five hours of spending time with one's own thoughts and emotions and with oneself. They would rather occupy themselves with entertainment and recreational activities because they are trying to avoid facing their true inner self. Shabbos is symbolic with bringing the *mikdash* into our own *mikdash me'at*, our own homes. We transform into a mini Beis Hamikdash. Lighting the candles is like lighting the *menorah*. The *avodah* of the *Mizbei'ach* is when we sit and learn and interact at the Shabbos table. The *Shulchan* with the twelve breads is the two *challos* on the table. The songs of the *Levi'im* are sung with the *zemiros Shabbos*. The *keruvim* are the experience of the family interacting and connecting.

The deeper meaning of *"Sheishes yamim ta'avod u'b'yom ha'shevii tishbos*—Six days you should work and on the seventh day you should rest," is that six days you should work on yourself and on the seventh day you should reflect on the person you have become. If all you are is a week older, you have missed the point of working that week. The Shabbos process is mirrored by the process of *shemittah*, which brings a person to *yovel*. During *shemittah*, you not only stop working on the land, you let go of what you own and you are left with what you are. You arrive at the seventh year, where you live only with your self and what you worked on throughout the week.

Parashas
Bechukosai

LIFE OF TORAH

I n *Parashas Bechukosai*, it speaks about the *berachos* and *klalos*; the *klalos* that will happen to Klal Yisrael if we don't keep the mitzvos. The *klalos* are mentioned twice in the Torah. Once, in *Parashas Ki Savo*, and here, in this week's *parashah*. We *lein Parashas Ki Savo* before Rosh Hashanah and this week's *parashah* we *lein* before Shavuos. In *Parashas Ki Savo*, we want to get rid of all the *klalos* before the new year—Hashem should end all the *klalos* and we should enter the new year full of *berachah*. This week's *parashah* speaks about the same idea: we want to get rid of all the *klalos* before the new year of Shavuos, the time of *kabbalas HaTorah*. This is also a new year. The same way we understand that Rosh Hashanah is a new year for *gashmiyus*, Shavuos is a new year for *ruchniyus*, for Torah. We want the *klalos* to end before the new year of Shavuos. Just like a person views his physical life as living, even more so, a person has to realize that Torah is *"ki heim chayeinu v'orech yameinu,"* life is Torah, and therefore we ask Hashem to end the *klalos* before.

The *sefer Yesodos B'Parashah* says that we should look at the *klalos* in *Ki Savo* and realize the reason for them is because there is a lack of

73

simchah. In the *klalos* in this week's *parashah*, the main point is *keri*, which means "happenstance." Just happening. The *klalos* in *Ki Savo* are talking about mitzvos that people don't do. So the main point there is that people have to do *mitzvos b'simchah.* This week's *parashah* is talking about Torah and those who learn it. There, Hashem demands that the Torah be learned with a *kevias itim* and not by chance. The *parashah* starts off, "*Im bechukosai teleichu,*" the *berachos* Hashem will give us if we go in His ways. Rashi explains that this means we should toil in Torah. *Chok* means with a set time, for example, "*Chok u'zeman nasan la'hem she'lo yeshanu es tafkidam.*" That can't be changed. When Torah is learned like that, we are on a whole different level.

Rav Shimshon Pincus explains that there is the *olam ha'gashmi* and *olam haTorah.* The *olam ha'gashmi,* this physical world, is where a person lives where there is a possibility that he will do *aveiros* and will deserve to be punished. When he lives in the *olam haTorah,* he is above the dictates of this world and then he can be *zocheh* to all the *berachos* and *arichas yamim.* What does it mean to live in the world of Torah? It doesn't mean to sit and learn the whole day, it means that he has a set time that he learns and during that time he cannot be disturbed and no one can get in his way. He is completely devoted to the Torah and that is his life at that moment. Such a person is living in the *olam haTorah,* a different world, and at that point he is able to be *zocheh* to all the *berachos.*

At the end of the *parashah,* we say, "*Chazak chazak v'nischazek.*" Reb Shmuel Brazil says that *chazak* refers to *chom,* the summer; *choref,* the winter; *zera* and *kotzer,* the time of harvesting and gathering in the wheat. All the different seasons of the year. A person should be *zocheh* that throughout the whole year he should be strong, able to commit himself to a life of Torah, and be *zocheh* to all the *berachos,* and a year of Torah and *hatzlachah.*

SEFER
BAMIDBAR

Parashas Bamidbar

DIVERSITY BRINGING UNITY

Them are two major points in this week's *parashah*.

1. The counting of Klal Yisrael.
2. When the Yidden traveled in the *Midbar*, they went in formation, in groups, with each *Shevet* carrying their banners.

These two points are connected. The *parashah* starts off, "*Se'u es rosh kol adas Yisrael.*" Hashem asks Moshe Rabbeinu to count Klal Yisrael. Rashi explains that "*mitoch chibosan*—out of love for Klal Yisrael," Hashem constantly counts them. This is like a person who has a treasure and constantly counts it out of love for that treasure. Hashem shows us how much He loves us, and He counts us and values each and every one of us and has *hashgachah pratis* over each individual. That is the counting of Klal Yisrael that the *parashah* starts off with.

The Torah continues with speaking about the *degalim*, the banners.

The midrash says that when Hashem brought the Torah down on Har Sinai, Klal Yisrael saw *malachim* come too and they were in a formation, carrying flags. Klal Yisrael craved the same thing. Hashem said to Moshe

Rabbeinu, "Klal Yisrael can also have *degalim*, flags, and each *Shevet* will have its own flag." Moshe was distressed because perhaps it would cause *machlokes* in Klal Yisrael. The flag points out each one's special *maalos*. A flag is raised to show your special qualities. Each group had its own special quality. Perhaps one *Shevet* would be jealous of another, causing *machlokes*. Hashem told Moshe, "Klal Yisrael have already had these formations for a long time." Yaakov Avinu had told the *Shevatim* how they should carry him. They therefore have these formations in them, and will be able to carry the flags.

Rav Eli Meir Bloch, Rav Yaakov Kamenetsky, and others explain that perhaps the cause of *machlokes* is when each one has their own *maalos* and special qualities and they think about themselves and put down the others. But if we are working together on a common goal and we are focused on that goal, we are like an army or band. In a band, each person has their own instrument that they play, but they are playing together to perform beautiful music. They realize that each one has their own specialty, but that the music won't come out so beautiful if they don't work together. Therefore, Klal Yisrael, after the *Mishkan* was erected, now has a common goal—they surround the *Mishkan* with their flags, and the focus is *avodas Hashem*. Therefore, even though there is diversity and each one has their own special qualities, they are all working together for one common goal—to serve Hashem. That will not cause *machlokes*.

Klal Yisrael is *"k'ish echad b'lev echad."* The *pasuk* says, *"B'shem elokeinu nigdal*—In the Name of Hashem we carry our banners." We raise our banners in the Name of Hashem and therefore there is *achdus*. The beginning of the *parashah* starts off with Hashem showing his love to us by counting us and pointing out how He loves each one specifically and watches over each one of us. Then we reciprocate by showing Hashem how we take our *maalos*, each one of us, and together we work to serve Hashem. *"B'shem elokeinu nigdal,"* we raise our banner and again show Hashem our love for Him. In this way we can come to *kabbalas haTorah* *"k'ish echad b'lev echad."*

Parashas Naso

THE BLESSING OF PEACE

דַּבֵּר אֶל אַהֲרֹן וְאֶל בָּנָיו לֵאמֹר כֹּה תְבָרְכוּ אֶת בְּנֵי
יִשְׂרָאֵל אָמוֹר לָהֶם: יְבָרֶכְךָ ה׳ וְיִשְׁמְרֶךָ: יָאֵר ה׳ פָּנָיו
אֵלֶיךָ וִיחֻנֶּךָ: יִשָּׂא ה׳ פָּנָיו אֵלֶיךָ וְיָשֵׂם לְךָ שָׁלוֹם:

This is how you shall speak to the B'nei Yisrael,
saying to them. "May Hashem bless you and
watch over you. May Hashem cause His Face
to shine to you and favor you. May Hashem
raise His Face toward you and give you peace."

(*Bamidbar* 6:23–26)

I n this week's *parashah*, there is the *birkas Kohanim*. It discusses
the *berachah* that the *Kohanim* give to Klal Yisrael. The *Ben Ish
Chai* explains the reason why, when people meet each other, they
stick out their hand to the other person and say, "*Shalom.*" What
is the reason for this? When one person meets another, he wants
to give him the biggest *berachah*. The biggest *berachah* we know is *birkas Kohanim*: "*Yevarechecha Hashem v'yishmerecha...*" There are fifteen
words in *birkas Kohanim*. A person has fourteen knuckles—each finger

has three knuckles and the thumb has two. This totals fourteen. When a person stretches out his hand to his friend he is giving him the fourteen parts of *birkas Kohanim*. Where is the fifteenth? The last word is *shalom*. So when you stick out your hand, you give the *birkas Kohanim*, to which you add *shalom*. Now you have the whole *birkas Kohanim*.

Perhaps on a deeper level, *birkas Kohanim* ends with the word *shalom*. The Gemara says, "*Ein lecha kli machzik berachah yoser min ha'shalom.*" In order for the *berachos* to come upon us, we need a vessel a *kli* to hold that *berachah*. There is no greater vessel for us to accept the *berachos* than *shalom*.

The hand is called a *yad*. When a person stretches out his hand, he reaches out to his friend's hand so there is *yad* connecting with *yad*. *Yud-daled* and *yud-daled* spells out *yedid* which is friendship. When we stick out our hand to another person, we are creating friendship, *shalom*. That creates the vessel for all the *berachos* to take effect.

The *pasuk* says, "This is the way you should *bentch* Klal Yisrael, *emor lahem*—tell them." What does it mean, "tell them"?

Rav Shlomo Levenstein says that the *Kohanim* tell the Yidden that "the *berachos* we give you are only fulfilled if you are worthy of them." We need to create that vessel so that the *berachos* should happen. That is *shalom*. This is why, when the *Kohanim* bentch Klal Yisrael, the *minhag* is that the people listening to it cover themselves with a *tallis*. It is not just that they shouldn't see the *Kohanim*'s hands, which are anyway covered with a tallis. Rather a person should take away all the distractions around them and should concentrate on accepting the *berachah* of *birkas Kohanim* and be that *kli kibel* of *birkas Kohanim*.

May we all be *zocheh* to have the full *berachah* of *birkas Kohanim*.

Parashas Behaalosecha

FEEL HASHEM'S SMILE
AND APPRECIATE IT

וַיֹּאמֶר מֹשֶׁה אֶל ה' לָמָה הֲרֵעֹתָ לְעַבְדֶּךָ וְלָמָּה לֹא
מָצָתִי חֵן בְּעֵינֶיךָ לָשׂוּם אֶת מַשָּׂא כָּל הָעָם הַזֶּה עָלָי:

Moses said to Hashem, "Why have You done
evil to Your servant; why have I not found
favor in Your eyes, that You place the burden
of this entire people upon me?"

(*Bamidbar* 11:11)

P erek 11 speaks about the Yidden who complained about
their situation in the *Midbar* and about their difficulties.
They especially complained about the *mahn*, and how
they wanted natural food, to the point that Moshe says in
pasuk 11, "*Va'yomer Moshe el Hashem lama hare'osa el avde-
cha*—Why are You being so bad to Your servant?" Why is it so hard? I
am trying to lead Klal Yisrael and all they do is complain. Then he says

in *pasuk* 15, "And if this is how You deal with me then kill me now." This is something that has never happened, that Moshe Rabbeinu should have such a reaction. Why is that?

Rav Dovid Steinhaus *al pi* Rav Avigdor Miller explains: Someone who complains about life and doesn't appreciate what Hashem does does not show gratitude, which is so essential to Klal Yisrael. For the *Shechinah* to rest in Klal Yisrael, the midrash *(Lekach Tov, Parashas Toldos)* says, *"Ein ha'shechinah sherua ela mitoch simchah*—The *Shechinah* will only rest if there is *simchah.*" When a person complains and doesn't appreciate everything Hashem does, he pushes away the *Shechinah*. It says in *Mishlei* (16:28), *"Nirgan mafrid aluf,"* someone who complains distances people from him. People don't like to be around someone who complains. The Gemara says in *Chagigah* 16a that *aluf* refers to Hashem, like *alef*, One and Only, *echad*. Hashem distances Himself from someone who complains and doesn't appreciate what Hashem does for him. Therefore, the *Shechinah* can't rest among a nation that complains. It is so essential to us as a nation and to each individual that the *Shechinah* rests among us.

Rav Moshe Tuvia Lieff points out that people spend 90 percent of their time complaining about the 10 percent that they lack and they spend 10 percent of their time appreciating the other 90 percent that they have.

Rav Shimshon Pincus says that at times we show gratitude to people but we don't have that natural gratitude to Hashem. This is because we don't perceive Hashem as a living, feeling Being. We perceive Him as remote and emotionless. One of the primary objectives in life is to correct this feeling. Our mission is to cultivate an emotional relationship with Hashem. The same way we perceive a regular human being and feel their kindhearted smile behind everything and every gift that they give us.

Rav Avigdor Miller brings down from the *Kuzari* that the reason why Hashem revealed Himself to the *Nevi'im* in a vision of a human being—as we see how sometimes the Torah speaks as Hashem in human terms like the feet, fingers, and ear—is because even though we may have a chance of making the mistake of thinking of Hashem as a human being, Hashem wants us to relate to Him as a human being and as a father and friend, to appreciate what Hashem does for us and feel

His love, and in that way maintain a relationship with Him. *Simchah* has the same letters as *machshavah*. *Simchah* is something that a person has to put his mind to. *Sameach* is *shin* and *mem*, which is "*sam*," while *mem* and *ches* is "*moach*." Put your mind to it and create the *simchah* and in that way, we will have Hashem's *Shechinah* rest with us.

Parashas Shelach

SEEING DEEPER

This *parashah* starts off with the *Meraglim* who were sent to look at Eretz Yisrael and to report back to Klal Yisrael about how good the land is. They failed and came back with a bad report. The end of the *parashah* is about the mitzvah of tzitzis: *"U'r'isem oso,"* look at the tzitzis, which remind us to do the mitzvos of Hashem. Both of these topics have to do with the the eyes and how to utilize our eyes.

The *Shelah* explains the difference between our eyes and ears. With the ears, there are sound waves going from outside into the ear. Eyesight goes out and it spreads. Since it spreads out and goes further and further, it means that the further it goes, the harder it is for the eyes to see. Glasses were made to limit the area that the eyes see and to bring it closer and help focus on the area. The eyes are meant to bring something closer to us. When the *Meraglim* came back, they said, *"V'hayinu b'eineinu k'chagavim*—We were like grasshoppers in the eyes of the giants." This is because they were so far away from them and therefore they looked small. The further away you are from something, the smaller it is. The closer you are, the bigger it is. Klal Yisrael are compared to the stars. The stars look small because we are so far away from them. The closer you get to them, the bigger you see it is.

When the spies gave their report, Klal Yisrael cried. Crying happens when a person feels distant from another person, where there is *richuk* (distance). The eyes bring close, and when you don't have that closeness, tears come out of the eyes. This is why Klal Yisrael cried when they heard the report—because of the distance they were from Eretz Yisrael.

The *Meraglim* didn't use their eyes to bring them closer to Eretz Yisrael, they didn't have a deeper look at what they saw, they only saw things on the surface.

Rav Moshe Shapiro says that in order to fix the *chet* of the *Meraglim*, the *parashah* of tzitzis was *nischadesh*. This mitzvah is to put tzitzis on our clothing. Rashi says that the word tzitzis comes from *"meitzitz min ha'charakim*—to look through a hole in the wall." That means not just to see something on the surface, but to focus and look deeper at what you see. This is the *tikkun* for the *chet* of the *Meraglim*.

The *pasuk* says, "You will see them [tzitzis] and you will remember all the mitzvos of Hashem." The Liska Tzaddik quotes from the Gemara in *Berachos* 9b, which says, "When do you start saying *Krias Shema?*" One of the opinions is that when a person sees his friend at a close distance of four *amos* and is able to recognize him. Only after that does the mitzvah of saying *Krias Shema* start. He explains a person might have thought that the mitzva of tzitzis—*"U'r'isem oso u'zechartem es kol mitzvos Hashem"*—is to remember all the *mitzvos bein adam l'Makom.* Says the Gemara, only after a person can see his friend up close does the mitzvah of *bein adam l'Makom* start. A person has to use his eyes to bring him closer to his friend, to realize he is a star, and therefore enhance his *bein adam l'chaveiro.* From there, he will learn to look at the mitzvos of Hashem in a closer way and it will bring him closer to Hashem, bringing him to remember all the mitzvos of Hashem and see Him clearly.

Parashas Korach

FOLLOW OUR LEADERS

This week's *parashah* speaks about the downfall of Korach and his followers who gathered together against Moshe. At the beginning of the *parashah*, in *pasuk* 3, the complaint was, "*Rav lachem*," Moshe and Aharon, you have enough power and leadership, "You have the *kehunah* and all of *malchus*, Klal Yisrael are holy and one," so why do you, Moshe and Aaron, seek the leadership? The mistake of Korach was that he thought unity means that everyone is on the same level. This is an incorrect way of viewing unity. Unity is like one body, a person. Klal Yisrael is "*k'ish echad b'lev echad*," a person. The whole body works together, but the body understands there is a leader and the head is the leader of the body. Without the head there would be total chaos. True unity can only be if we follow our leader. If a person follows his *rebbi* then he has the guidance and he understands what to do and the correct way. The reason for this is because our *manhigim*, the *talmidei chachamim* of the *dor* who learn the Torah, which is *emes*, truthful—they know the true way of serving Hashem. If a person wants to grow, he needs the leadership and guidance of a *rav*, *rebbi*, and *gadol ha'dor*. They have the true way of viewing how we should live our lives. We may have ulterior motives in what we do, but the leaders of Klal Yisrael are *emes*, they learn *Toras emes* and they have no ulterior motives. They have no *negios*, and they tell us the true way of living.

Korach's punishment was that the ground opened up and swallowed him and his followers alive. The Mishnah in *Avos* says that you must have *moreh malchus*, respect of authority, and if not, "*Ish es r'eihu chayim v'lo*—A person would swallow his friend alive." There would be no true unity. Only with the guidance of *gedolim* can we work together as a group and can Klal Yisrael exist. Therefore, Korach, who disagreed with this, and his followers were swallowed alive. As the Mishnah says, "*Ish es r'eihu chayim v'lo*." This is the reason they were punished in this way.

How did Moshe prove Korach wrong?

He took the stick of Aaron and it grew. Korach said that the whole nation is *kulo kedoshim*, they are all holy. The way he was viewing the nation was that they were all holy, but they won't grow that way. The Torah says, "*Kedoshim tehiyu*—you must grow in *kedushah*." The way to grow is if you follow the leaders of Klal Yisrael. So Aharon's stick grew. *Pasuk* 23 says, "*V'hinei parach mateh Aaron*." *Parach* has the same letters as *chafar*—*ches, peh, reish*. The opposite of Korach, which was *chafar*, "dug in the ground"—Aaron was something that grew, *parach*. "*Emes mi'eretz titzmach*—The truth will grow from the ground." The midrash (*Tanchuma, Parashas Korach, siman* 11) says that Korach and his congregation say from under the ground, "*Moshe emes v'toraso emes*." Perhaps this is why, on Simchas Torah, the day we accept the Torah *b'simchah*, we jump up and sing, "*Moshe emes v'toraso emes*"—we are growing, not like Korach who is dug underground. We follow our leaders and that is how we grow and that is why we jump and sing, "*Moshe emes v'toraso emes*."

Parashas Chukas

BECOME CLOSER TO HASHEM THROUGH TEFILLAH

This week's *parashah* speaks about the Yidden who complained about the *mahn*. They despised it and they wanted regular food. Hashem punished them with snakes that bit them, and they got sick. Moshe then made a statue of a snake out of copper. Copper, *nechoshes*, is similar to the skin color of the snake. *"V'hibit nachash nechoshes va'yechi*—If they looked at the snake they would live." Why did they get punished with a snake bite because they complained about the *mahn*? What is the connection? Why was the cure in the form of looking at a snake?

Birkas Shimon explains that the Yidden complained about the *mahn* because they wanted to live a regular life, acquiring their food through their own work instead of the *mahn* falling down from *Shamayim* every day. The *nachash* by Adam HaRishon was punished by having the legs that the snake used to have removed. Now the snake has no legs and has to crawl on the ground. In a way, that's a *berachah* for the snake because now it has easy access to its food at all times. The fact is it was really a curse for the snake. As long as it doesn't have food accessible, the snake has to look up and ask Hashem for food. If the snake has food the whole time it has no reason to connect with Hashem. This is Hashem's way of distancing the snake.

Klal Yisrael wanting to have regular food acquired by their own hands was a way of avoiding the connection with Hashem. With the *mahn*, they had to re-ask Hashem each day for the next day's food. Every day they were connecting with Him. This is the greatest thing and it's what Hashem wants. Therefore, they were punished by the bite of a snake, which doesn't connect with Hashem everyday and is distant from Him. Their *refuah* was that when they looked at the snake, using their eyes in the correct way, not just seeing the snake but seeing past it—understanding what the snake represents and that the greatest thing for a person is to be connected to Hashem, speak to Hashem, and daven to Him every day.

It says in *Tehillim*, "*Kirvas Elokim hi tov*," what's good for me is being close to Hashem. What does it mean to be close to Hashem? To always be connected to Him through our *tefillos*. Each month in the Jewish year is related to a different part of the body. Tammuz is related to the eyes. We saw last week that the *Meraglim* didn't use their eyes in the correct way. In this *parashah* we see that the *refuah* for Klal Yisrael was when they looked at the snake. That look is a deeper look—to see the message of the snake, which is to be connected to Hashem and to be close to Him. Through our *tefillos* every single day we connect with Hashem and we should be *mechazek* in our *inyan* of *tefillah* always.

Parashas Balak

FOCUS ON THE GOOD IN OTHERS

וַיֹּאמֶר אֵלָיו בָּלָק לְכָה נָּא אִתִּי אֶל מָקוֹם אַחֵר
אֲשֶׁר תִּרְאֶנּוּ מִשָּׁם אֶפֶס קָצֵהוּ תִרְאֶה וְכֻלּוֹ לֹא
תִרְאֶה וְקָבְנוֹ לִי מִשָּׁם:

Balak said to him, "Come with me to another
place from where you will see them; howev-
er, you will see only a part of them, not all of
them and curse them for me from there.

(*Bamidbar* 23:13)

I
n this week's *parashah*, King Balak wants Bilaam to come and
curse Klal Yisrael: "*Lecha na iti el makom acher asher tirenu…*" Balak
asks Bilaam to come with him to a place where he will see part of
Klal Yisrael, but not all of them.

What was the thought process of Balak, that he only wanted
Bilaam to see part of Klal Yisrael?

The *Sefas Emes* explains that it says in *Pirkei Avos* (1:6), "*Hevei dan es kol adam l'chaf zechus*—Judge the whole person favorably." Why does it say "*kol ha'adam*"? He explains that at times a person can look at somebody and see that he did wrong, he did *aveiros*. But if you look at the whole person, generally he is a good person. We focus on the little things a person does wrong and judge them accordingly. The Mishnah says we should judge *kol ha'adam*, to indicate that we should look at the whole person. On the whole, they are good people. This is what Balak wanted from Bilaam. Come and look at least at part of Klal Yisrael. Klal Yisrael on the whole are good and you are not going to be able to curse them. Focus on just part of them or on just a few people and then you will find bad and be able to curse them.

Further on in the *parashah* (23:21), we find what Bilaam did say, "*Lo hibit oven b'Yaakov*." Rashi explains, "*Lo ra'ah amal b'Yisrael*," Hashem doesn't see any bad Klal Yisrael does, "*Hashem elokav imo*." The Shinover Rav explains it differently: "*Lo hibit oven b'Yaakov*." The *Mishnah* in *Avos* says, "If you look at the whole person, they are good." If you focus on the small parts, the bad of the person, you will see bad.

"*Lo hibit oven b'Yaakov*," a person should not look at the bad of Klal Yisrael or of a specific person. Don't focus on that. *Hibit*—you see it but you ignore it. You look the other way. Look at the good of the person. "*V'lo ra'ah amal b'Yisrael*," is an even higher *madreigah*. Don't even see. But even if you are not holding there, look the other way, look at the *maalos* of Klal Yisrael or a specific person.

The *Divrei Chaim* says that at the end of the *pasuk* it says, "*Hashem elokav imo*—Hashem is with you." If you are a person that doesn't look at the bad of Klal Yisrael or of a specific person, but sees the good and focuses on it, then Hashem says, "I am with you."

When you have a little dot on top of another dot at the end of a *pasuk*, it looks like a *yud* on top of a *yud*. If you have one Yid on top of another Yid, that's the end, its a stop. But if you have one Yid next to another Yid, one can look at the other and they are together—that makes up the *Shem Hashem* and Hashem is there. "*Hashem elokav imo*," Hashem is with us when we focus on the good of ourselves, of others, and Klal Yisrael.

May we be *zocheh* that in this *zechus*, the fast of Shivah Asar b'Tammuz should be a Yom Tov instead of a fast day.

Parashas Pinchas

THE YOM TOV
OF THE THREE WEEKS

he *Ohev Yisrael*, the Apter Rav, says that in this week's *parashah* we read about all the *Yamim Tovim*. He asks, "Why do we read about these happy days during the period of the Three Weeks?" If you count the *Yamim Tovim* including Shabbos, which is one day, Rosh Chodesh, one day, Sukkos, eight days, Pesach, seven days, Rosh Hashanah, two days, and Yom Kippur, which is one day, you get a total of twenty-one days. Like the twenty-one days of the Three Weeks. The *pasuk* in *Tehillim* (31:20) says, "*Mah rav tuvcha asher tzafana l'rei'echa*—How great are You Hashem Who has hidden the goodness for those who fear You?"

Hashem hid the goodness of the Three Weeks. They are essentially good days. The goodness is hidden until Mashiach comes, when they will be revealed. The source of the twenty-one days of Yom Tov is in the Three Weeks. Their light comes from these three weeks, but it is hidden. When Mashiach comes, these three weeks will be days of Yom Tov, starting with Shivah Asar b'Tammuz and all the intermediate days will be like *chol ha'moed*. The last day of Yom Tov will be Tishah b'Av. Not only that, but Tishah b'Av will be the greatest of all the *Yamim Tovim* and the father, *av*, of all the *Yamim Tovim*.

The Mezeritcher Maggid explains that these three weeks are called *bein ha'metzarim*. "*Kol rodfeha hisiguha bein ha'metzarim*," those who run after Hashem can reach Him in this period of *bein ha'metzarim*.

A *mashal* for this is that when a king is in the palace, it is very hard to see him and to get an audience with him. When he is out of his palace, it is much easier to speak to him and connect with him. When Hashem was in His palace in the Beis Hamikdash, it was hard to reach Him. Now that it is destroyed and He is out in the open, it is easier to connect with Him and get close to Him during this period of time, the *bein ha'metzarim*.

Rav Yaakov Emden says that the source of all our *tzaros* in this *galus* is because we don't mourn for the Beis Hamikdash. We don't feel its loss. We don't observe the laws of *aveilus* for the Beis Hamikdash correctly. If we would be together with yearning for the Beis Hamikdash and anticipating Mashiach, this would bring the *geulah*. Not only that, but if we mourn for the Beis Hamikdash, that would be the reason to rejoice because we would be connecting to the light of the rebuilding of the Beis Hamikdash.

The Rizhener points out that if we look at the *parashah*, between all of the *Yamim Tovim* there is a letter *samech* separating one Yom Tov from the next. This means "*stuma*," closed up. Between Shavuos and Rosh Hashanah, there is a *peh*, which means "*pesucha*," it is open. There will be no other *Yamim Tovim*, except between Shavuos and Rosh Hashanah. Tishah b'Av will turn into a Yom Tov—it will be a new Yom Tov, so it is left open for this Yom Tov.

We should be *zocheh* to observe these Three Weeks and turn them into good days and be *zocheh* to see Mashiach, *bimheira b'yameinu*.

Parashas Matos

PROTECTING OURSELVES

The end of the *parashah* speaks about the six *arei miklat*. A person who kills accidentally has a place to run to—six cities—and save himself and not get killed. The Apter Rav asks, "Everything in the Torah has to apply at all times. How do the *arei miklat* apply in our day?" *Arei miklat* are places for a person to run away to if he did a sin. Today, if a person does an *aveirah*, where can he run to? Six *arei miklat* are *keneged* the six words of "*Shema Yisrael Hashem elokeinu Hashem echad.*" If a person wants to run away from his *yetzer hara* to a safe place, he runs to these words. The Gemara says that an *eitzah* for a person who does *aveiros* is to say *Krias Shema*. *Shema Yisrael* is being *mekabel ol malchus Shamayim*. A person has to be reminded twice a day that the only *eitzah* to run away from the *yetzer hara* is to be connected to Hashem.

These Three Weeks, we have three *haftoros*. One starts with "*Divrei Yirmiyahu,*" the second is "*Shimu,*" and the third is "*Chazon.*" "*Divrei*" is speaking, words. "*Shimu*" is listening, and "*Chazon*" is seeing. These are three things we need to work on: speech, listening, and seeing. This week's *parashah's haftarah* is *"Shimu*—Listen." Like *Shema Yisrael*, which means to listen.

Each of the twelve months corresponds to a different part of the body. *Chodesh* Av corresponds to the ears—listening. The *Meraglim* did an *aveirah* and Klal Yisrael listened to their *lashon hara*. What does it mean? It doesn't mean just to hear the words. *Shema* means to connect to the person or the being that is speaking. The only way to connect is by listening with your heart. When we say *Shema* and accept Hashem as king, we want to connect to Hashem. Hashem is always there sending messages—He is talking to us throughout the day. We need to hear the message that Hashem is sending. Hearing is done when we put our minds and heart to what is being told to us, and we listen to and internalize the message—then we connect to Hashem. That is why there is an *ir miklat* for the *yetzer hara*.

This is a month of working on our listening to another person. When someone has a *tzarah* and we listen and put our heart into trying to understand him, that is connecting to the person and it uplifts the person. The same too when it comes to *ol malchus Shamayim*.

In the Gemara in *Shabbos*, it says: "Yerushalayim was destroyed because they didn't say *Krias Shema* of *Shacharis* and *Arvis*." Saying *Krias Shema*, listening and connecting with Hashem, and hearing His messages will protect us from the *yetzer hara* throughout the day. *Im yirtzeh Hashem*, we should be *zocheh* to the *binyan bayis bimhera b'yameinu*.

Parashas Masei

BUILDING THE RELATIONSHIP

This week's *parashah* speaks about the travels of Klal Yisrael in the *Midbar*.

Rav Aharon David points out that when the Torah speaks about the creation of the world, it does so in thirty-four *pesukim*. When the Torah speaks about Har Sinai, it takes thirteen *pesukim*. *Krias Yam Suf* is spread over thirteen *pesukim*. When the Torah speaks about the challenges of Klal Yisrael in the *Midbar*, it uses forty-four *pesukim*, more than any other situation or event in the Torah. Why does it get so much attention? At the beginning of the *sedrah*, Rashi brings a *mashal* comparing this to a king who had a sick son. They were traveling to a faraway place to try and heal him. After he was healed, on their way back, the father pointed out to him everything that had happened in the different places on their travels. What is the purpose of the king relating their travels and what happened in each place?

Rav David says that a true relationship is not a business partnership where two sides are working together to a common goal. Rather, it is two sides that are sharing their life together. The king was reminiscing with his son about their experiences and all that they had gone through; it was a conversation to build the relationship between the two of them. This is a *mashal* of the relationship between Klal Yisrael and Hashem. Hashem was relating to Klal Yisrael what happened in each place. This was reminiscing, forging the relationship between Klal Yisrael and Hashem.

Rav David says we can apply this concept to the relationship between husband and wife. Marriage is not just two people sharing a common roof. Rather, they are sharing their lives and experiences together. Perhaps this is the reason why the *baal korei* sings when he *leins* the travels of Klal Yisrael. Rather than looking at these years of traveling in the desert to Eretz Yisrael as difficult years, they were the years when we forged our relationship with Hashem. This was of utmost importance for Klal Yisrael. This is the joy of these years. We became a special nation through these journeys and therefore we sing the *masa'os*. This is the way a couple should spend their lives, spending time with each other, building their relationship, whether through reminiscing, or sharing their experiences or feelings. If Hashem views this as a worthwhile investment and spends so much time in the Torah on pointing out this important *yesod*, then certainly we should do the same.

SEFER

DEVARIM

Parashas Devarim

HOW TO REBUKE WITH LOVE

Sefer Devarim is the last *sefer*. The first *pasuk* says, "*Eileh ha'devarim asher diber Moshe el kol Yisrael*—These are the words that Moshe said to all of Klal Yisrael."

As Rashi points out, Moshe Rabbeinu is coming now to say *mussar* and *tochachah* to all of Klal Yisrael. There are times that a person has to give *mussar* to somebody else. What is the proper way of giving *mussar*? We learn many lessons from Moshe in how to give *mussar*. *Ha'devarim* means "words." Some *mefarshim* say that it has the same letters as the word *devorim*, "bees." Bees sting but they also produce honey. When it comes to giving *mussar*, which can be something that stings, one has to do it in a way that is sweet like honey. If we look at the *pesukim*, Moshe Rabbeinu doesn't say directly what Klal Yisrael did wrong. He says it in a hinted way. He mentions the places where they did the *aveirah*, but he doesn't mention the *aveirah*. When it comes to giving *mussar*, you don't attack the person directly. You speak about the thing that is wrong and the person realizes that he did something wrong. This is one lesson.

Another thing is that Moshe said this *mussar* to all of Klal Yisrael, including himself, too. Moshe Rabbeinu spoke to himself and Klal Yisrael heard it. He was giving *mussar* to himself and from there, Klal Yisrael heard that there was something wrong. It was not an attack on them. He was speaking about himself in order not to hurt their feelings.

Later in the *parashah*, in *pasuk* 12 when Moshe says, "*Eichah esah levadi tarchachem*," How can I carry your burden, all the fights that there are among Klal Yisrael? I am going to have to appoint "*anashim chachamim nevonim u'yedu'im*." Moshe says, "You are going to have to have special people, you are such a *chashuve* nation, you need special people to judge you." The *pasuk* says, "*V'hayaveka chacham v'yaveka*—When you give *mussar* to a *chacham*, he will love you." The *mefarshim* say that when you give *mussar* to somebody, call him a *chacham*—you are a special and smart person. For you it is not appropriate the way that you are behaving. Raise him up and he will love you for that *mussar* and he will go with the *mussar* and listen to it too—because you said it in a way that was sensitive to his feelings.

The *gematria* of the word *mussar*—mem, vav, samech, reish—is 306. *Devash* is also 306. When a person gives *mussar*, it should be said in a sweet way. That way the person who hears it will be able to accept it and do it.

Let's learn from Moshe Rabbeinu to be sensitive to others and in this way, it will bring us together and we will be *zocheh* to the *geulah shleimah*.

Parashas Va'eschanan

KRIAS SHEMA

In this week's *parashah* is the *Shema*. When we say *Shema*, we cover our eyes and concentrate on being *mekabel ol malchus Shamayim*. Why do we have to cover our eyes, why can't we just close our eyes and concentrate like that?

Rabbi Ephraim Stauber explains that every person's hand is unique. There are no two fingerprints alike in the entire world. Everyone has their own unique fingerprint. A person takes his hand and puts it over his eyes and he has to know that when he is being *mekabel ol malchus Shamayim*, there is a specific, unique way for him in his *avodas Hashem* that no one in the entire world has. He has to have his own special *kabbalas ol malchus Shamayim*.

How does a person know what that is? It says in the *parashah*, "*V'ahavta es Hashem elokecha b'chol levavecha*—You should love Hashem with all your heart."

Levavecha is in the plural. Are there two hearts?

B'chol levavecha means "*im shnei yitzrecha*," with both the *yetzer hara* and the *yetzer hatov*.

How do we serve Hashem with the *yetzer hara*? This is the opposite of *avodas Hashem*.

103

In *Alei Shur*, Rav Shlomo Wolbe brings down from Rav Tzadok Hakohen that when a person has a weakness in his *avodas Hashem*, for example with his *berachos*, it is where he has his weakness that lies his greatest *hatzlachah* and the greatest potential for growth. The *yetzer hara* attacks the person *davka* in that area because it knows that there lies his success. So if a person wants to know, he should look at the *yetzer hara*, take the *yetzer hara*, and see where he lacks in his *avodas Hashem*. Then he knows that if he puts his *kochos* into there, he will have the greatest potential for *hatzlachah*. This is what is meant by "*b'shnei yitzrecha*."

Reb Moshe Feinstein asks, "Of course you serve Hashem with the *yetzer hatov*?" A person sometimes thinks that a certain act is good. This is not necessarily the case. He needs to find out from his *rebbi*, *rav*, or guide if this is the proper way to act, even when it seems good. He needs the Torah to guide him. This is what it means to serve Hashem with the *yetzer hatov*.

From Tishah b'Av until Sukkos is sixty-five days, which is the same *gematria* as *alef, daled, nun, yud*, the *Shem Hashem* which is also sixty-five. From Tishah b'Av until Rosh Hashanah is fifty days, that is *nun*. From Rosh Hashanah until Yom Kippur is ten days, that is *yud*. Yom Kippur until Sukkos is four days, *daled*. Sukkos—"*U'l'kachtem lachem b'yom rishon*"—is one. A total of sixty-five days. After Tishah b'Av starts the *avodah* of being *mekabel ol malchus Shamayim*. We understand now where to put our *kochos* into.

"*Nachamu nachamu ami yomar Hashem elokeichem*," Hashem says that now is the time for *nechamah*, to rebuild. You have that *Shem Hashem*. The *Eibeshter* is with us, helping us to rebuild the *nechamah*, to be *mekabel ol malchus Shamayim*. May we be *zocheh* to the true *nechamah*—Tzion.

Parashas Eikev

ONE JEW, ONE MITZVAH, ONE DAY

וְהָיָה עֵקֶב תִּשְׁמְעוּן אֵת הַמִּשְׁפָּטִים הָאֵלֶּה
וּשְׁמַרְתֶּם וַעֲשִׂיתֶם אֹתָם:

And it will be, because you will heed these
ordinances and keep them and perform them.

(Devarim 7:12)

I t says in this week's *parashah*, "*V'hayah eikev tishma'un*—If a person will listen." The midrash says that *eikev* is a *lashon* of "the end," like the heel of a person. The head is the beginning and the heel is the end. "If a person will listen to the Torah at the end." What does this mean? The *mefarshim* explain that this part of the year is at the end of the year. It is after Tishah b'Av and before Elul and Rosh Hashanah, the new year. In this part of the year, people tend to be more relaxed in their *avodas Hashem*. The *pasuk* says, "*v'hayah*," which is a *lashon* of *simchah*. *Eikev* means that at the end of the year a person also needs to listen to the ways of the Torah like the rest of the year. The way a person can attain this always is by being a "*tishme'un*," and listening to the ways of the Torah.

The *pasuk* says in 18:1, "*Kol ha'mitzvah asher anochi metzavecha ha'yom tishme'un la'asos*—All the mitzvos that I command you today, you should do."

Watch! There are three problems in this *pasuk*.

The *pasuk* says, "*Kol ha'mitzvah*"—it sounds like there is only one mitzvah, but there are many mitzvos.

The *pasuk* continues, "*asher anochi metzavecha*." Metzavecha is *lashon yachid*. Is there only you yourself and nobody else?

The *pasuk* says "ha'yom." Is it only today that you have to do the mitzvos. Not tomorrow?

The *Mateh Yehudah* explains that the Torah is giving us a way of how to act in life. Sometimes a person has a mitzvah to do and he thinks, "Why do I need to do this mitzvah? There are many other mitzvos." A person has to know that if he has a mitzvah to do at this moment, he should make believe that there is no other mitzvah, just this one mitzvah. Another thing, don't push off a mitzvah to another day. Make believe that this is the only day you have to do this mitzvah, and there is no other day. The third thing is to know that if a mitzvah comes your way, don't say "Why do I have to do this mitzvah? There are many other people that could do this mitzvah?" A person has to view it like he is the only person in the world.

The Chafetz Chaim used to say that there is only one person in the world, one day, and one mitzvah. If a person views life this way, then it will be a *tishme'un*.

This may be what the *pasuk* means later on when it says (10:12), "*V'atah Yisrael mah Hashem elokecha sho'el mei'imach ki im l'yirah es Hashem*." Now and no other day. A *lashon* of *yachid*—Hashem is asking you and nobody else. "*Ki im l'yirah*." Im is a *lashon* of *miyut*, Hashem is asking you one thing, one mitzvah for you to do and no other mitzvah today—and you are the only one to do it.

If a person views his *avodas Hashem* this way, it will be a *tishme'un* and the year will end off in a way of *simchah*.

Parashas Re'eh

OPEN YOUR HANDS

כִּי יִהְיֶה בְךָ אֶבְיוֹן מֵאַחַד אַחֶיךָ בְּאַחַד שְׁעָרֶיךָ בְּאַרְצְךָ אֲשֶׁר ה' אֱלֹקֶיךָ
נֹתֵן לָךְ לֹא תְאַמֵּץ אֶת לְבָבְךָ וְלֹא תִקְפֹּץ אֶת יָדְךָ מֵאָחִיךָ הָאֶבְיוֹן: כִּי
פָתֹחַ תִּפְתַּח אֶת יָדְךָ לוֹ וְהַעֲבֵט תַּעֲבִיטֶנּוּ דֵי מַחְסֹרוֹ אֲשֶׁר יֶחְסַר לוֹ:

If there will be among you a needy person, from one of
your brothers in one of your cities, in your land Hashem,
your God, is giving you, you shall not harden your heart,
and you shall not close your hand from your needy
brother. Rather, you shall open your hand to him, and you
shall lend him sufficient for his needs, which he is lacking.

(*Devarim* 15:7–8)

I n this week's *parashah*, the *pasuk* says, "You should not harden
your heart or close your hands from your brother who is poor.
You should open up your hand to him." This is talking about the
mitzvah of *tzedakah*.

The Dubno Maggid asks why the mitzvah of *tzedakah* is

different from all other mitzvos in that the *pasuk* has to say, "*Lo sikpotz es yadcha*—Don't hold yourself back from doing the mitzvah." It doesn't say this when it comes to shaking the lulav or other mitzvos. Why is this different? With all other mitzvos involving spending money, it is your money that you are spending. When it comes to *tzedakah*, it is not your money that you are spending. Hashem gave you the money for the purpose of the poor person. It is the poor person's money. You are just like the bank teller holding on to the money for the poor person. Hashem is entrusting you to hold onto it for him and when the time comes that he needs it, to give it to him. It is his money. That is why the Torah has to tell us not to harden our heart when it comes to this mitzvah because a person is to know that it is not his money he is spending, it is the poor person's money. The word *kesef* is spelled using the letters *kaf*, *samech*, and *peh*. The letter before *kaf* is *yud*. The letter before *samech* is *nun*. The letter before *peh* is *ayin*: this spells out the word *ani*. The *ani* preceeds the *kesef*. When a person has money, he has to know Hashem already prepared the poor person before he got the money, for him to give that money to the poor person.

The *Sar Shalom* of Belz says that a person has to know that he has to give, even though it is difficult for him to do so. When a person closes his hand, making a fist, notice that all the fingers are the same. When you open your hand, you see your fingers are different sizes. When a person holds himself back and doesn't give, he views everybody as the same, there is no reason to give one person over another. A person has to open his hand and see that there are different people, different needs—some people need more, others need less, and your heart should be open to give it to them. A person shouldn't feel that he is losing out by giving. The *pasuk* says, "*Aser t'aser*," a person should give *maaser* in order that they should become rich. Hashem looks to give to those good people who hold onto their money for the poor, and then give them more. If you take the word *t'aser*. Take a tenth of the first letter, *taf* (400) which is forty. A tenth of *ayin* (70) is seven. A tenth of *shin* (300) is thirty. A tenth of *reish* (200) is twenty. Forty is *mem*, seven is *zayin*, thirty is *lamed*, and twenty is *chaf*. This makes the word *mazlacha*, "your mazal," which all depends on how much *maaser* you give. You give *tzedakah*, your *mazal* will be that you have more money because Hashem sees He can trust you to give to the *ani*.

Ashir—*ayin, shin, yud, raish*—equals 580. *Ani*—*ayin, nun, yud*—equals 130. The difference between *ashir* and *ani* (580 minus 130) is 450, which is *"tein"*—*taf, nun*. The difference between somebody who is rich and poor, is that the one who gives, it's not so much how much he has, but he is the *ashir*, the *samei'ach b'chelko*. This is who the Torah considers an *ashir*.

Parashas Shoftim

THREE WAYS OF TESHUVAH

לֹא יָקוּם עֵד אֶחָד בְּאִישׁ לְכָל עָוֹן וּלְכָל חַטָּאת
בְּכָל חֵטְא אֲשֶׁר יֶחֱטָא עַל פִּי שְׁנֵי עֵדִים אוֹ עַל פִּי
שְׁלֹשָׁה עֵדִים יָקוּם דָּבָר:

One witness shall not rise up against any
person for any iniquity or for any sin,
regarding any sin that he will sin. By the
mouth of two witnesses, or by the mouth
of three witnesses, shall the matter be
confirmed.

(*Devarim* 19:15)

The *pasuk* says, "When testifying against someone who does an *aveirah*, you need at least two or three witnesses to testify." The *Ben Ish Chai* finds a *remez* in this *pasuk* to the *inyan* of teshuvah. He says, "The word *eid* is a *remez* to *teshuvah*. *Eid* is a *tachshit*, an adornment, a piece of jewelry. *Teshuvah* is a jewel that we have, that Hashem gave to each and every person to purify themselves.

There are three ways of doing *teshuvah*: *teshuvah*, *tefillah*, and *tzedakah*. The *Ben Ish Chai* says that everyone can do at least two of these three easily. *Teshuvah* and *tefillah* every person can do. *Tzedakah* might be difficult to do. Therefore, the *pasuk* says, "*Al pi shnei eidim yakum.*" At least two of the *eidim*, of these two adornments, two ways of doing *teshuvah*, a person can do. "*O al pi sheloshah*—Sometimes three also." The best is all three ways of doing *teshuvah*. So if it is hard, a person can do two of the three ways of doing *teshuvah*. But the best is to do all three.

Earlier in the *parashah*, in 17:7, it says, "*Yad ha'eidim tihiyeh bo b'rishonah.*" The brother of the Maharal, Reb Chaim, in his *Sefer HaTiul* asks why when a person says, "*Selach lanu,*" do we take our fist and pound our heart? He explains that the *pasuk* in *Iyov* says, "*Yad kol adam yachtom,*" a person's hand signs on all his *aveiros*. We also say in the *Mussaf* of the *Yamim Nora'im*, "*V'chosem yad kol adam bo.*" Hashem has a ledger of a person's mitzvos and *aveiros* and the person's own hand signs that ledger. When a person does an *aveirah*, he has a way of rectifying it and that is through the mitzvah of *tzedakah*. The *pasuk* in *Daniel* says, "A person can do away with his *aveiros* if only he would give *tzedakah*."

The *Arizal* says, "This is why we pound our hearts. We are so stubborn and we close our hand, we make a fist and we don't give *tzedakah*. If only we would give *tzedakah*, Hashem would give away our *aveiros*."

"*Selach lanu avinu,*" we pound our hearts. It is because we closed our hands and fists and didn't give *tzedakah*. For that, the *aveirah* still exists. The only way of getting rid of the *aveirah* is by giving *tzedakah*. This is the way of absolving our *aveiros*.

We should be *zocheh* now that Elul is coming and we are preparing for the *Yamim Noraim*, to do all three ways of *teshuvah*, *tefillah*, and *tzedakah* and be *zocheh* to a good year.

Parashas Ki Seitzei

ANI L'DODI V'DODI LI

כִּי תֵצֵא לַמִּלְחָמָה עַל אֹיְבֶיךָ וּנְתָנוֹ ה׳ אֱלֹקֶיךָ בְּיָדֶךָ:

When you go out to war against your enemies,
Hashem, your God, will deliver him into your hands.

(Devarim 21:10)

The *pasuk* says, "*Ki seitzei l'milchamah al oivecha u'nesano Hashem elokecha b'yadecha*—When you go out to war against your enemies, Hashem will deliver him into your hands."

Rav Yaakov Singer points out that it seems from the *pasuk* that as soon as you go to war, right away Hashem will give your enemies into your hands.

How do we reach the understanding that as soon as we go out to war, we will win the war?

The last letter in the word *ki* is *yud*. The last letter in *seitzei* is *alef*. The last letter in *l'milchamah* is *hei*. The last letter in *al* is *lamed*. The last letter in *oivecha* is *chaf*.

So you have *alef, lamed, yud, hei, chaf.* If you spell that out it says, "*elokecha.*" If, when you go out to war, you are taking *elokecha,* Hashem, with you then immediately you will win the war and Hashem will put your enemies into your hands. You might take this a step further.

The *Ohr Hachaim* says that "when a person goes out to war" refers to the biggest enemy we have, the *yetzer hara—oivecha.* When you go out to war against the *yetzer hara,* if you go out to war with Hashem and take Him along with you in the war against the *yetzer hara,* then right away, "*u'nesano Hashem elokecha b'yadecha,*" you will win the war and you will succeed in overpowering him.

Parashas Ki Savo

BEGINNING THE YEAR

The *tochachah* in this week's *parashah* speaks about the tragedies—the punishments Hashem will bring to Klal Yisrael in the future—for not keeping the Torah and the mitzvos. In 28:47, we learn the reason we will be deserving of these punishments: *"Tachas asher lo avadeta es Hashem elokecha b'simchah u'v'tuv leivav u'b'rov kol,"* because we didn't serve Hashem with *simchah*.

Rav Shlomo Levenstein says in his *sefer* that it is understandable for a person not to be *b'simchah* during the week. The week is hard, he is working; there is stress and he is busy. But when it comes to Shabbos, our day of rest, when we are not busy and can connect with Hashem, then a person has no excuse not to be *b'simchah*. At least on Shabbos, a person should serve Hashem *b'simchah*. This is what the *pasuk* means to say. *"Tachas asher"*—*tachas* also means "under." Look under the word *asher*—*alef, shin, raish*. The letter after *alef* is *beis*. The letter under *shin* is *taf*, and the letter under *reish* is *shin*. *Shin, beis, taf* is Shabbos. *"Tachas asher"*—if you look under the word *asher*, it is Shabbos. If on Shabbos, a person is not *b'simchah*, for that we are worthy of the *tochachah*. Shabbos is our day when we should totally serve Hashem *b'simchah*.

Parashas Nitzavim

HASHEM NEVER GIVES UP ON US

וַיִּתְּשֵׁם ה׳ מֵעַל אַדְמָתָם בְּאַף וּבְחֵמָה וּבְקֶצֶף גָּדוֹל
וַיַּשְׁלִכֵם אֶל אֶרֶץ אַחֶרֶת כַּיּוֹם הַזֶּה:

Hashem removed us from our land in anger,
with fury, and great wrath, and He threw us
to another land, as this very day.

(*Devarim* 29:27)

"V a'yishtem Hashem mei'al admasam b'af u'b'chemah u'b'ketzef gadol—Hashem removed us from our land in anger, v'yashlichem el eretz acheres ka'yom ha'zeh—He threw us to a different land as this very day." The *lamed* in *va'yashlichem* is an extra long big *lamed*.

The *Ridvaz* explains the significance of this long *lamed*. "*Va'yashlichem el eretz acheres*—Hashem will throw us to other lands." If a person has

115

a wallet and he throws it into the street, he is showing that he is not interested in the wallet; it is *hefker* and anybody can come and take it. It is not his anymore. The halachah says that if someone throws a wallet into the street but it has a string attached to it and the string is also attached to the person who threw it, even though he threw it into the street, it is not *hefker*. The fact that there is a string attached to him and to the wallet shows that even though he threw it to the ground, he is not giving up on it, he is not making it *hefker*, it is still his. The *Ridvaz* says that the *pasuk* is telling us that even when we do *aveiros* and Hashem is going to throw us out of our land to other lands, don't ever think that Hashem is giving up on us and letting us go. There is always that string that is attached to us and Him. The big *lamed* goes all the way up from us to Hashem. Even when He throws us away, He never gives up on us. He is always attached to us and always holding on to us, connected to us.

This is a lesson for us as we approach this coming Shabbos, Erev Rosh Hashanah, the beginning of a new year. Sometimes a person feels lost, "Maybe Hashem gave up on me because of my *aveiros*," or whatever the reason may be. A person should never despair. He has to know that whatever *matzav* he may be in, Hashem never gives up on us or leaves us. He is always attached to us ready to help us up once again, to be close to Him.

Parashas Vayelech

REALIZING OUR DISTANCE

וְחָרָה אַפִּי בוֹ בַיּוֹם הַהוּא וַעֲזַבְתִּים וְהִסְתַּרְתִּי פָנַי מֵהֶם וכו׳
וְאָמַר בַּיּוֹם הַהוּא הֲלֹא עַל כִּי אֵין אֱלֹהַי בְּקִרְבִּי מְצָאוּנִי
הָרָעוֹת הָאֵלֶּה. וְאָנֹכִי הַסְתֵּר אַסְתִּיר פָּנַי בַּיּוֹם הַהוּא עַל
כָּל הָרָעָה אֲשֶׁר עָשָׂה כִּי פָנָה אֶל אֱלֹהִים אֲחֵרִים:

Hashem says, "On that day I will be angered with Klal
Yisrael and I will leave them and I will hide My Face from
them. And it will be said on that day, 'Why did all these
bad things happen? Because Hashem is not among us.' I,
Hashem, will hide myself doubly on that day."

(Devarim 31:17–18)

T he *pasuk* says, "Hashem says, "On that day I will be angered
with Klal Yisrael and I will leave them and I will hide my face
from them." Klal Yisrael said on that day, "Why did all these bad
things happen? Because Hashem is not among us." It says in
the next *pasuk*, "I Hashem will hide Myself doubly on that day."

The question is, if we follow the *pesukim*, it first says that Hashem will hide Himself from Klal Yisrael and Klal Yisrael will say, "Why is this happening to us? Because Hashem is not among us." It gets worse. Hashem says, "I will hide Myself doubly." Klal Yisrael recognized that Hashem was not with us, so why were they then punished with, "*Anochi haster astir panai ba'yom ha'hu.*"

There are many answers. Rav Shlomo Levenstein explains that when bad things happen to us and a person thinks, "Why is this happening?" he comes to the conclusion that Hashem is not with us and he stops by that. This is not what Hashem wants. Hashem wants us to take it a step further: Why did He leave us? Why is He not among us? There must be something we are doing that is lacking. What can we do to bring Hashem back closer to us?

Here is a *mashal* from the *Ohr Daniel*. There was a person who was working on solving the world's problems. His young son came over to him and said, "I want to come up with an answer too." He was bothering his father, so the father got upset and took a map of the world and cut it up into pieces. He gave it to his son and said to him, "You try and put this together and then we will talk." Not long afterward, the son came back to his father with the map completed. The father was surprised and asked him how he did it? The son replied, "I don't know how to put the world together but I flipped over the pieces you gave me and there was a picture of a person. I know how a person looks, so I put together the pieces of the person and now I have the world fixed." The *Ohr Daniel* says that this is what a person should be doing. When we have problems in the world, to solve the world's problems is not something we can do. But each person knows what he has to fix in himself and he should look into that. When a person fixes his problems, the world's problems will be fixed. When Klal Yisrael has *tzaros*, each individual has to look into his own situation.

The *pasuk* says that if a person doesn't do this then the punishment is *haster astir*. The Baal Shem Tov says that this punishment of hiding means that we will be so lost, we won't even realize that Hashem is hiding Himself. If we realize Hashem is hiding and that we are distant from Him there is a way for us to return. But Hashem says, "I will hide Myself so that you won't even realize that you are so far away from Me." Then there is no *eitzah* for getting close because we don't realize we are far.

Even then, Hashem says that there is an *eitzah*. The following *pasuk* says, "*V'atah kisvu lachem es ha'shirah ha'zos*," which is referring to the songs—the Torah. Even when He hides himself, if we look into the Torah and learn the Torah, we will see how to get close to Hashem even though we are so far.

There are thirty pesukim in this week's *parashah*, which represent the thirty days of Elul, a time when we can do *teshuvah* and, *im yirtzeh Hashem*, we should be *zocheh* to do a *teshuvah sheleimah*.

Parashas Haazinu

WE ARE THE PORTION OF HASHEM

כִּי חֵלֶק ה' עַמּוֹ יַעֲקֹב חֶבֶל נַחֲלָתוֹ:

Because Hashem's portion is His people,
Yaakov, the lot of His inheritance.

(*Devarim* 32:9)

The *Tanna d'bei Eliyahu* says that one of the *middos* of Hashem is that He is *samei'ach b'chelko*, happy with His portion. Rav Chaim Volozhin asked his *rebbi*, the Vilna Gaon, what this means as the whole world is His—He doesn't have a portion. The Vilna Gaon answered him with a *pasuk* from this week's *parashah*, "*Ki chelek Hashem amo*—Hashem's nation (Klal Yisrael) is His portion. Sometimes, Klal Yisrael is not on the *madreigah* they should be and we don't act the way we should be either. Since we are His portion, He is happy with us no matter the stage or *madreigah* we are on. Even when we fall low, Hashem is happy with us. He loves us and will never forsake us. This is what the *pasuk*, "*Ki chelek Hashem amo*," means and it is what the *Tanna d'bei Eliyahu* means when it says that Hashem is always happy with His *chelek*. He is always happy with us, no matter the *madreigah* we are on. He always loves us and will never forsake us.

Parashas Ve'zos HaBerachah

THE BLESSING OF FORGETTING

לְעֵינֵי כָּל יִשְׂרָאֵל:

Before the eyes of all Yisrael.

(*Devarim* 34:12)

The last words in this week's *parashah* are *"l'einei kol Yisrael."* It refers to Moshe Rabbeinu's strength that he had in front of all of Klal Yisrael. Rashi says that, going back in time to when the Yidden were dancing around the *egel* and Moshe threw down the *Luchos* he was holding, breaking them, *"V'ashaber l'eineichem"*—Hashem agreed to what Moshe did. The *pasuk* says, *"Asher shibarta yasher kochacha."*

Why is this the last *pasuk* in the Torah? Why is the message that the Torah has to end off with the strength of Moshe—that he broke the *Luchos*?

Rav MosheTuvia Lieff answers this question. The *Yalkut Shimoni* says that had Moshe not broken the *Luchos*, Klal Yisrael would never have forgotten the Torah. *Shichechas haTorah* only happened after the *Luchos* were broken. What are the thanks for breaking the *Luchos*? The thanks are because without forgetting Torah, we would just learn the Torah and remember it. We wouldn't have the toil of repeating and repeating the Torah until we master it. It would not become part of us. "*Ashrei adam oz lo bach*—happy is the person where the Torah is within him." We can learn Torah, but it only becomes part of us with *ameilus b'Torah*. This, we would have missed had it not been for Moshe breaking the *Luchos*. Now that he broke the *Luchos* and we have *shichechas haTorah*, with *ameilus* the Torah can become part of us. Happy is the person where Torah is part of him. Perhaps this is the reason why we dance on Simchas Torah, at the end of the Torah. Just like Moshe broke the *Luchos* when the Yidden were dancing around the *egel*, today on Simchas Torah we dance around the *Sefer Torah* because now we have acquired that fascinating idea of *shichechas haTorah*, which causes us to be *omel b'Torah*—this is the *simchas haTorah*.

"*Adam l'omal yulad*—a person was created to toil." This leads us into *Parashas Bereishis*. The purpose of the creation of Adam was to toil. It says in the Gemara that a person can toil for worldly matters or for Torah. *Ashrecha*, happy is the person that his *ameilus* is in Torah. This is the connection between *Ve'zos HaBerachah* and *Bereishis* and it gives us the strength to toil in Torah.

We should be *zocheh* to a year of remembering what we learned and the Torah should become part of us.

YAMIM TOVIM

Rosh Hashanah

The *Ben Yehoyada* points out an outlook to life's challenges, how to overcome and face them.

He says that when we have situations in life which are hard and difficult and we might look at them as bad, we call it a *chov* in Hebrew. The *gematria* of chov—*ches, vav, beis*—is eight, six, and two, which equal sixteen. We can look sometimes at a *chov*, but we can turn it into *tov*, which is the *gematria* of seventeen. *Tov* is one more than *chov*. A person can take *chov* and turn it into *tov* if he adds one, by adding to his situation the One and Only, the Ribbono Shel Olam, *echad*.

The *pasuk* in *Tehillim* 14:3 says, "*Ein oseh tov gam echad.*" Sometimes, we ask a person how things are and he says that it is not going good, "*Ein oseh tov.*" Therefore, "*Ein gam echad,*" because he doesn't have the *echad* with him—he is not looking at the situation with the *echad*, Hashem. If he has *echad*, it is *tov*.

In the Rosh Hashanah davening, we say "*V'chol maaminim.*"

The *Chasam Sofer* says that this *tefillah* goes according to the *alef-beis*. It talks about praises of Hashem. One is "*Ha'chosech chaim l'chol chai*—Hashem apportions life to all the living." *Chosech* can also mean "cut." Let's *chosech*, "cut," the word *chaim*. The *gematria* of the word *chaim* is 68. Let's cut *chaim* in half; this becomes 34, which is *lamed* and *daled*. If you switch these letters around it says *dal*. Hashem sometimes wants a person to live. He wants *chaim* for a person, but he is not deserving of it. Hashem wants him to live so He makes him poor. An *ani* is considered *k'meis*. An *ani* is a *dal*. So Hashem will make a person poor in order that he can have life. "*Ha'chosech chaim l'chol chai*," Hashem will cut *chaim*, take the 68 and cut it in half, making the person poor in order that he should live. Sometimes when a person sees a situation, he might think it is *chov* but in reality it is *tov*. A person can take the *chov* and if he has Hashem with him, realizing that Hashem is always there, doing everything for him, he can take the situation and turn it into *tov*.

We should be *zocheh* this year to have a *shanah tovah u'mesukah*, we should see how everything Hashem does is good for us, turn the year into a sweet year, and be *zocheh* to a *kesivah v'chasimah tovah*.

Yom Kippur

We say in *tefillah Zakah*, the *tefillah* before *Kol Nidrei*, "In the *zechus* of the *tefillos* we are going to daven on this day of Yom Kippur, they should go up and they should join with them all the *tefillos* we davened thoughout the year without *kavanah*, and Hashem should accept all our *tefillos* through the *tefillos* of Yom Kippur.

Sefer Amen tells about a person who didn't come to shul for many days. The Chortkover Rebbe called him in and asked why he didn't come to shul. He told him that he has a problem—he wants to daven with *kavanah*, and he tries day after day to do so, and he never succeeds. So he stopped davening, because davening without *kavanah* is like not davening. The Chortkover told him he was making a mistake. The *pasuk* says *(Tehillim* 87:6) that "Hashem counts like the *goyim* write." He explains the *pasuk*: if a person davens and doesn't succeed doing so with *kavanah*, then in *Shamayim*, Hashem puts it down as a zero. If the same thing happens the following day, it is marked with a zero again. The same thing repeats itself the next day too. Each day that he tries to daven with *kavanah* but doesn't succeed is marked down with a zero. Let's say after ten days he finally succeeds, then that is a one. If a person davens thoughout the whole year without *kavanah*, and it comes to the day of Yom Kippur and he has the proper *kavanah*, Hashem puts it down as a one. Where does He place the one? By Yidden we count from right to left. *Goyim* count from left to right. The *pasuk* says, "Hashem counts like the *goyim* write, which means from left to right. So Hashem puts the one on the left of the zeros. Now, if you have a whole year without *kavanah*, and each day, Hashem put a zero, that is 364 zeros. If he has *kavanah* on Yom Kippur, Hashem puts the one before the zero. So that is one with 364 zeros after it. A massive amount that he has acquired with that one *tefillah b'kavanah* that he has on Yom Kippur. This is what the *pasuk* means. Never give up and never feel like not trying. Every time we try is worth it, because at the end when you succeed, all those zeros become part of that one. This doesn't apply just by Yom Kippur, but any mitzvah that we try, like *lashon hara*, Shabbos, learning. Never give up trying. Every time you try, even if you don't succeed, at the end when you do succeed all those times you tried join together and become a massive amount of a mitzvah.

As we approach Yom Kippur, we should try as hard as we can to have the right *kavanah*, have all those zeros joining and, *im yirtzeh Hashem*, this year Hashem should hear all our *tefillos* from each member of Klal Yisrael, and be *zocheh* to a *gemar chasimah tovah*.

Sukkos

The Gemara brings down three different ways of building the walls of a sukkah. It can be built with four walls, three walls, or two walls and a *tefach*. These three ways are hinted to in the word sukkah. The word sukkah is spelled *samech, chaf,* and, *hei. Samech* is a circle, it covers all four sides. A *chaf* is three lines, it covers three sides. The *hei* is two and a bit lines, like the two walls and a *tefach*.

There is a *sefer* from Rabbi Moshe Gersht. He explains from the *Arizal* the three different ways of building a sukkah. Sukkos is a time when Hashem shows us how much He loves us. We come to Yom Kippur full of *aveiros*. On Yom Kippur, Hashem forgives us. After Yom Kippur, Hashem wants to show that not only does He forgive us, but He loves us even more. The *Arizal* brings down the *pasuk* in *Shir HaShirim* 8:3, "Hashem's left hand is under my head and His right arm embraces me." The *Arizal* explains that on Sukkos, Hashem brings us into his sukkah—He gives us His hug. There are three ways a person can give a hug. When a person faces someone and puts his arm completely around him, a bear hug. This is one way of building a sukkah, where it is surrounded on all four sides.

Another way of giving hug is to face the person and take your two arms and put them around his arms. Now he is surrounded by you from three sides—that's a sukkah from three walls.

Another way to hug is when you are standing side-by-side with another person and you take your arm and you put it over his shoulder and your hand around his arm. He is surrounded by you from two sides. The hand around his arm is that *tefach* that surrounds him. These are the three ways a person can show a hug, and these are the ways Hashem says, "I am showing you my love." This is the love Hashem shows us. We can add that we show Hashem and reciprocate our love for him. On Sukkos, we take the lulav and esrog and encircle the *bimah* where the *Sefer Torah* is being held. We are showing that our focus is Hashem and our love for Him is solely to Him, nothing else. So he shows us His love, His focus, and we show back our love to Him, that He is our focus. This the specialty of this Yom Tov—*Zeman Simchaseinu.*

Shemini Atzeres and Simchas Torah

We are now coming to the end of Sukkos—Shemini Atzeres and Simchas Torah.

Rav Shimshon Pincus says in the name of *mekubalim* that the order of the *Yamim Tovim* starts with Pesach and ends with Shemini Atzeres. He explains why the order is especially this way. The first Yom Tov is Pesach, the time when Hashem took us out of Mitzrayim and made us into His nation. "*Atah vechartanu*," He chose us as His nation. This was like the birth of Klal Yisrael. Therefore, this is the first Yom Tov. After this comes Shavuos. A baby is born, he grows up, he develops, and becomes bar mitzvah. On Shavous, we got the Torah and it was like the bar mitzvah for Klal Yisrael. Then comes the stage when a person gets married, *nisu'in*. This corresponds with Sukkos. The sukkah is like a *chuppah* that we stand under together with Hashem. It is a *zeman simchaseinu*, like a *chasunah* is a *simchah*.

We can add that on Sukkos, we hold the lulav and we put rings on it. The lulav is like a stick which points straight, like the finger of the *kallah* which she sticks out to get the ring from the *chassan*. The lulav is pointing up to Hashem, our *chassan*.

The next stage is Hoshana Rabbah, when we go seven times around the *bimah* with the Torah in the center. Just like in Yericho when Klal

Yisrael went seven times around the wall to bring down the wall that separated them from the city. There is still a separation between us and the Eibeshter, so we go seven times around the *bimah* where the *Sefer Torah* is to break down the barriers and to bring us closer to Hashem. This is the *chuppah* where the *chassan* is getting closer to the *kallah*.

After Hoshana Rabbah comes Shemini Atzeres. This, Rav Pincus says, is the time when Hashem says, "I want to spend time just with Klal Yisrael, alone." Like the *chassan* and *kallah* in the *yichud* room after the *chuppah*. Now they are alone. Shemini Atzeres is when we spend time with Hashem and with no other nation.

We can take this a step further.

After Shemini Atzeres comes Simchas Torah. After the *chuppah* and *yichud*, the *chassan* and *kallah* dance. Simchas Torah is the time when we dance with the *Sefer Torah*. We dance with the *kallah*. This is the next stage of Klal Yisrael when we dance with the *chassan* and *kallah*. We hold onto it and hug it.

Then we finish with the *Yamim Tovim*. Often, we feel after Yom Tov is over that it is just finished. This is not true. The *simchah* is just beginning. Just like at a *chasunah*, that is just the beginning of the *simchah* between *chassan* and *kallah*. It continues. They live together and that is the main *simchah* for the *chassan* and *kallah*. After Simchas Torah, we go to the further stage of *simchah*, we live together with our *chassan*. We take the Torah and learn it, and when we learn we are actively living together with the Eibeshter, our *chassan*. The *simchah* continues throughout the winter.

Purim

There are many mitzvos to be done on Purim day. One of the mitzvos is *mishloach manos*.

Rabbi Daniel Katz says that during the time of Esther and Mordechai, Haman came to Achashveirosh and said that the Jews deserve to be killed. He mentioned that they are a scattered nation, *"Am mefuzar u'mefurad."* Chazal say that at this time the *achdus* in Klal Yisrael was not so strong. That means that in order for Esther to counteract Haman's decree, all the Jews had to gather together, *"Lech kenos kol ha'yehudim."* They had to strengthen their *achdus* and unity, which would counteract the anger that Haman has against Klal Yisrael. For this reason, we have the mitzvah of *mishloach manos*, sending presents to our friends and neighbors to add to our *achdus* and unity.

Sinas chinam is not what we think—hating for no reason. We don't hate anybody for no reason, we always have a reason why we hate somebody. *Sinas chinam* is that the reason we hate someone is not a valid reason. We have to do the opposite, *"V'ahavta l'rei'acha kemocha,"* we have to love our friend. What does *"v'ahavta l'rei'acha"* mean? The root of the word *ahavah* is *hav*, which means "to give." When you give to another person you add love to the other person, because you are giving of yourself and expanding yourself to the other person. Now that other person has a part of you. The love you have for yourself now extends to the other person. There is more to it.

"*V'ahavta l'rei'acha.*" *Rei'acha* is your friend. It could have said *chaver-cha*. When someone dislikes another person, he finds in him wrong and bad. For this reason, he hates him. If a person would really look at himself, he would also see things he does that are bad, yet he loves himself. Why? For himself, whatever he does wrong he will always have an answer, reason, and explanation why it is not so bad. He can love himself even though he has these things he does that are bad. This, a person will do for himself. But a person has to use the same love for himself and extend it to his friend. The root of the word *rei'acha* is *reish, ayin. Rei'ah* is a friend, but *reish, ayin* can also mean "bad." The mitzvah of *v'ahavta l'rei'acha* is that the same way you love the bad in yourself, *l'ra cha*, that is the way you should love your *rei'ah* too—love and accept your friend's bad too, *kemocha*, like your own. If you can do it for yourself, you can extend it to your friend. This is the mitzvah of *v'ahavta l'rei'acha.*

This is the mitzvah of "*mishloach manos ish l're'eihu,*" not "*l'chavercha.*" Even if a person can find something *ra* that he dislikes in the other person.

Rav Yerucham Levovitz says that the mitzvah of *mishloach manos* is *b'ikar* to those whom you may not get along with and have something that disturbs you. There is no reason not to like such a person. You should give them the *matanah*, the *mishloach manos l're'eihu*, to add the *ahavah* to such a person. That is the mitzvah of *mishloach manos.*

We should be *zocheh* to be *mekayem* this mitzvah together with all the other mitzvos of Purim.

Pesach

DIVREI TORAH ON THE SEDER

Yachatz—we break the middle matzah. The three matzos represent *Kohen, Levi,* and *Yisrael.*

Why do we break the middle matzah, which is *Levi*? It's brought down about the *shibud* in Mitzrayim that the Yidden who went down to Mitzrayim were Yaakov and the *Shevatim.* The Yidden did not have to start working until the last of the *Shevatim* died, which was Levi. After Levi died, they started working hard in Mitzrayim. We take the *Levi*-matzah and break it in half, showing that once Levi died, the *shibud* started.

~~~~~~

The *Chasam Sofer* says that the reason we have an egg on the *ke'ar-ah,* which some people have the *minhag* to eat, is because in order to make a hard-boiled egg one puts the egg into water on the fire and it cooks. The more it is under the fire, the harder it will become. That is the same with Klal Yisrael. The harder we had to work in Mitzrayim, the more we produced, and the greater we became. "*K'asher ya'anu oso kein yirbeh v'yifrotz,*" the more the Mitzriyim made it hard for us, like putting us under the fire, the more we grew. Klal Yisrael grows under pressure. We are in *galus* and the more pressure there is, the stronger we become.

~~~~~~~~~~

Rav Zalman Sorotzkin asks why the Yidden had to leave Mitzrayim after 210 years. We know they were in a rush to leave Mitzrayim because we know that if they would have stayed longer, they would have fallen to the fiftieth *shaar* of *tumah*, so they had to be rushed out of Mitzrayim.

Why are we today in *galus* for over two thousand years and we are existing and there is no threat to us, while in Mitzrayim they had to leave after 210 years or they would have fallen to the fiftieth level of *tumah*? In Mitzrayim, they had no Torah; the only thing they had going for them was that they didn't change their names, clothing, or language. That was good and they were able to last for 210 years. After the Yidden got the Torah on Har Sinai, we were able to last much, much longer and we are therefore able to be in *galus* for over two thousand years without it being a threat to our existence.

~~~~~~~~~~

We say, "*V'hi she'amda l'avoseinu v'lanu, she'lo echad bilvad omad aleinu l'chaloseinu*—There wasn't just one nation that got up against us to destroy us," yet Hashem saved us from them.

The *Sefas Emes* says, "*She'lo echad bilvad*," this alone, that Klal Yisrael were not one, not together, is a reason why "*amad aleinu l'chaloseinu*—the nations of the world rose up against us." That alone is enough reason for us to be destroyed. Yet, Hashem saved us. Why? "*She'lo echad*," the *goyim* are not together in destroying us because they can't get together as one, and therefore we were saved. Had they been together with the same idea to destroy us, we would have been destroyed. Hashem made sure that they were not together—and that alone saved us—because He loves us.

~~~~~~~~~~

In *Tzei U'lemad*, we speak about Lavan Ha'Arami. Why do we speak about Lavan and what does he have to do with Pharaoh and Mitzrayim? The *Mahari Bei Rav* says that the truth is that Yaakov was supposed to marry Rachel. The first son of Rachel was Yosef. Had he been the first son, he would have been the *bechor* and the brothers wouldn't have been jealous that Yaakov treated him special. Since Lavan switched Leah for Rachel, Yosef wasn't the firstborn and therefore, when Yaakov treated him special and gave him the *kesones pasim*, the brothers were jealous: Why should he be better than them if he's not the *bechor*? Because of the jealousy, they sold him to Mitzrayim and therefore we went down to Mitzrayim. So it was all Lavan's fault that we went down to Mitzrayim; had he not switched Rachel for Leah, the brothers wouldn't have been jealous and we wouldn't have gone down to Mitzrayim.

Pesach Seder

The end of the Seder is *Nirtzah*. The last two parts of *Nirtzah* are *Echad Mi Yodei'a* and *Chad Gadya*. We need an explanation as to what they are about and why they are at the end of the Seder.

Rav Avrohom Gurwicz explains *Echad Mi Yodei'a* as follows: The night of the Seder is a night of *emunah* when we instill in ourselves *emunah* in Hashem in His control and power of the world and how good He is, how he takes care of us. We speak about *yetzias Mitzrayim*, the *nissim*, and *krias Yam Suf*. We eat matzah and *maror*. The whole night is a night of *emunah*. At the end of the Seder, we want to test a person to see if the *emunah* had the proper effect on him, if it changed him. There is a game called "word association"—what is your first reaction, your thoughts to a word said. At the end of the Seder, we test a person. When a person says the word one, our first reaction should be, "One is Hashem." If the night had its proper effect on us, that is our proper reaction to "What is one?" When we hear the word "two," our reaction should be, "Two is the *Luchos*." Then we know that the Seder had its proper effect on us.

The next part of the Seder is *Chad Gadya*. Rav Moshe Wolfson explains that we start off *Chad Gadya* with a goat that was eaten by a cat. The cat was wrong for eating the goat, the goat was innocent. The dog that ate the cat was correct because the cat was wrong for eating. The stick was

140

wrong for hitting the dog. The fire was right for burning the stick. The water was wrong for putting out the fire. The ox was right. The *shochet* was wrong. The *malach ha'maves* was right, but then Hashem killed the *malach ha'maves*. Why did Hashem kill the *malach ha'maves*? If we follow the steps, everything he did was right? It seems so to say that Hashem did something wrong. We want to end off the Seder with this question. With *emunah*, a person has no questions. Without *emunah*, a person has no answers. We want that a person should walk away from the Seder with the question of, "Why did Hashem kill the *malach ha'maves*?" and he should not be bothered by the question. We know from the end of the night if it had the proper effect on us. We know that Hashem is in control and He does good, everything is with a *cheshbon* and everything is right. It is no question why Hashem killed the *malach ha'maves*, we are not bothered with the question. With proper *emunah*, we have no question. This is the way a person should leave the Seder. This is the way we know that the Seder had its proper effect.

Nirtzah means "will." *Nirtzah* is Hashem's will. At the end of the Seder, we want Hashem's will to be that He wants us. The *Imrei Emes* used to say about *Chad Gadya*, that *gadya* is from the *lashon* of *haggadah*, "to say." What does it mean "*chad gadya*—one saying"? Hashem, we are waiting for Your one *haggadah*. You said a saying that You are going to take us out of this *galus*. We know a *klal* that "once a person says something, he cannot retract his words." We end off *Chad Gadya*—"Hashem, You said You are going to take us out of this *galus*. Please keep that *haggadah* that You said." Perhaps this is why the whole Seder is called "*haggadah*." To remind us of "His word" that He is going to take us out of this *galus*. We say our *haggadah*, and we ask Hashem to say His *haggadah* of taking us out of this *galus*. We did our *kezayis* of matzah and *maror*. Please Hashem, You do Your *kezayis* of *Nirtzah*, wanting us and taking us out of this *galus*.

Shevi'i
Shel Pesach

The last day of Pesach, *shevi'i shel Pesach*, the day of *krias Yam Suf*, we *lein* "Az Yashir," the *shirah* Moshe Rabbeinu and Klal Yisrael said at the *yam*.

Why did Klal Yisrael say *shirah* only by *krias Yam Suf*, and not at the end of the *makkos* in Mitzrayim or at *yetzias Mitzrayim*? *Sefer Atah Vechartonu* explains that they did thank Hashem after *yetzias Mitzrayim* for the *nissim*, but *shirah* is a different *madreigah*. *Shirah* was said when they realized what they thought was bad was actually good. When the Mitzriyim were running after them, it seemed bad but in retrospect, it was really good for them. They ran after them in order to get drowned in the *Yam Suf*. After *krias Yam Suf*, they realized that what they thought was bad was really good, and when they realized that, they said *shirah*.

The *Sefas Emes* explains that the word *shirah* has two roots: *shir*, which is the same letters as *yashar*, straight. *Shirah* comes from "*shirim u'nezamim*—bracelets and earrings." He explains that a bracelet is circular, round. A circle starts at a point and then the line starts sloping downward as if it is leaving its point and going down. Then it turns around back up and meets the point where it started. So what seems as if it is leaving its source and going down is really part of the process of

142

going back up and returning and making a full circle, meeting up with where it started. This brings out the *inyan* of *shirah*—when something seems like it's bad, leaving its source, but is really part of the process of good. This brings a person to *shirah*. This is the *yashar*—a *niggun*. A song is made up of a high and low, and together it comes out as one beautiful song. It needs the high and the low, which is all one part of the *yashrus*. It is really all straight.

"*Az yashir.*" It doesn't say, "*shar,*" that they sang. Rather, it is in the future, "they will sing." A person has to know that he is always to look and to sing *shirah*. How does he attain this if we don't always see that the bad is good? It says in the *pesukim*, "*V'yaaminu b'Hashem u'b'Moshe avdo,*" they believed in Hashem and after that, "*az yashir.*" When you have *emunah*, you believe that what looks bad is really good, and then you can come to say *shirah*.

The matzah is a round circular shape. It is called the "food of *emunah*." The matzah infuses us with *emunah*. It is that round circle—once we have *emunah*, we will be able to say the *shirah* which is round, and we should be *zocheh* to say the *shirah* of Mashiach.

Shavuos

The *Midrash Yalkut Shimoni* in *Parashas Bamidbar* says that when Hashem gave the Torah to Klal Yisrael, the nations of the world were jealous and wanted to know why they were *zocheh* to the Torah over them. Hashem said to them, "Show Me your *sefer yuchsin*, the book of your lineage." The midrash continues that the reason why Klal Yisrael were *zocheh* to the Torah was because of their *sefer yuchsin*; they have the book of their lineage. What does this mean?

Rav Yosef Volofi says that there is a midrash that the Torah was given with three things: fire, water, and the *midbar*. There are three times Klal Yisrael did an act of *mesiras nefesh*.

1. Avraham Avinu went through fire, the *kivshon ha'aish*, and was *moser nefesh* for Hashem.
2. Klal Yisrael went through the *Yam Suf* and were ready to *moser* their lives for Hashem—they were ready to drown.
3. The Yidden went into the desert, *eretz lo zarua*, a place of danger. Yet they were ready to go and follow the word of Hashem.

Three times—fire, water, and *midbar*. This is our lineage. Because of this we were *zocheh* to *kabbalas haTorah*, because of our power to be *moser nefesh* for Hashem. "*Naaseh v'nishma*," we were ready to give everything for whatever He says. Because of this we received the Torah. There was the fire at Har Sinai and there was the *anan*, the water dripping from the skies at *kabbalas haTorah*. We received the Torah in the *midbar*. In the *zechus* of these three acts of *mesiras nefesh* we were *zocheh* to the Torah. Perhaps we can add a little more.

The *Mahari* says that there are three things we learn from the fire, water, and desert. When it comes to doing mitzvos, a person has to use his passion, the fire within him, to do the mitzvah with *zerizus*. He should do the mitzvah with true *simchah* too. This is the fire.

The water—sometimes when it comes to *aveiros* and things we shouldn't be doing and the *yetzer hara* is trying to convince to us to do them, we need to act cold, like water, and not listen to his convincing ways. There we have to act with the *middah* of water, to be cold.

The *midbar*—at times we have people around us who discourage us from doing mitzvos and learning Torah and they speak *lashon hara*. In these situations, a person has to seclude himself from such people, and be like in a *midbar*, away from them. Don't be convinced by the people around you to do the wrong thing. These three ways that the Torah was given, through fire, water, and desert, are the ways that we have to act.

Im yirtzeh Hashem, we should be *zocheh* to an *emesdik kabbalas haTorah*.

Tishah B'Av

Tishah b'Av—we mourn the Beis Hamikdash. We start at night and continue during the day, sitting on the floor and saying *kinnos*. We do this until *chatzos*, when we get up and sit on a regular chair. The *paroches* that was taken off is put back on. We put on tefillin. We say, "*nacheim.*" We act differently from the afternoon time onward. This is strange because the actual Beis Hamikdash that was destroyed and burned started burning in the afternoon and carried on until the next day, the tenth of Av. Why is it this way? Why at the time when the Beis Hamikdash burned do we start acting in a more joyful manner?

Rav Sokolov explains that on the day of Tishah b'Av, in *Shamayim*, they were judging who should be destroyed. Should Klal Yisrael or the Beis Hamikdash be destroyed? Hashem decided that out of His love for Klal Yisrael He can't destroy them and would rather destroy His own home, the Beis Hamikdash. He would rather go into *galus*, instead of Klal Yisrael.

The Romans came into the Beis Hamikdash and saw the *Aron* with the *keruvim*. The Gemara in *Yoma* 54b says that when Klal Yisrael sinned, the *keruvim* didn't face each other. When Klal Yisrael were doing the *ratzon Hashem*, they faced each other. When the Romans entered, they found the *keruvim* were hugging in an act of love. At this moment, Hashem was showing Klal Yisrael how much He loves them. He is ready to give up His own home in order that they should be saved. Therefore, at this point in the day we start acting in a more joyful way, because we realize how much Hashem loves us.

Tishah b'Av is called a *moed*. It will be the greatest *moed* because there is no Yom Tov that Hashem shows His love to this extent to Klal Yisrael. The month that Hashem destroyed the Beis Hamikdash is called Av. This is the month Hashem shows love like a father to a son. It goes further. When it was hard to see Hashem, the place He could be seen was in the Beis Hamikdash. Now that Hashem destroyed it, He is showing us that He is out in the streets and we can see Him even among the darkness, where we would not have seen Hashem in the past. He is out there for us, showing His love. Av—*alef, beis*—stands for "*Elul ba*—Elul is coming." This month of Av precedes the months of Elul and Tishrei. Tishrei, Rosh Hashanah, is a time when we accept Hashem as our king, *malkeinu*. We have to know that before *malkeinu*, Hashem is *Avinu*: "*Avinu Malkeinu*." Av comes before Tishrei because we first have to know how much love Hashem has for us. That He is our Father, our King.

May we be *zocheh* that this Tishah b'Av should be the Yom Tov of Tishah b'Av and we should be *zocheh* to the *geulah shleimah bimheirah b'yameinu*.

About
the Author

Rabbi Yosy Munk grew up in Brooklyn, NY, and learned in Yeshiva and Mesivta Torah Temimah. During his *beis midrash* years, he continued his learning by Rav Meir Stern, *shlita*, and developed a close relationship with Rav Mordechai Schwab, *zt"l*, the Mashgiach of the Passaic yeshiva. He also learned in Yeshivas Bais Hatalmud in Bensonhurst and heard *shmuzen* from Rav Shlomo Brevda, *zt"l*. Together with his wife, the daughter of Rav Moshe Possick, *shlita*, from Torah Umesorah, Rabbi Munk moved to Lakewood, NJ, and he learned in Beth Medrash Govoha for eighteen years. He joined Rabbi Avraham Mordechai Newman, *shlita*, in Yeshiva Mayan Hatorah, where he serves as a *sho'el u'meishiv* and has had the opportunity to develop a strong connection with the *bachurim* and grow together with them. Rabbi Munk has been sharing *divrei Torah* with the students every Friday for the last twelve years.

Rabbi Munk is a grandson of Rav Eliyahu Munk, *zt"l*, who was a Rav in Paris and wrote many *sefarim*, including the classic English commentary on the siddur, *World of Prayer*, and *Kol HaTorah* on Chumash. His grandfather was a tremendous inspiration for him.